INTERSECTIONALITY IN ACTION

INTERSECTIONALITY IN ACTION

A Guide for Faculty and Campus Leaders for Creating Inclusive Classrooms and Institutions

EDITED BY

Brooke Barnett and

Peter Felten

Foreword by Eboo Patel

1996-2016 20ᵀᴴ ANNIVERSARY

Stylus
PUBLISHING, LLC.

STERLING, VIRGINIA

Published by Stylus Publishing, LLC
22883 Quicksilver Drive
Sterling, Virginia 20166-2102

Library of Congress Cataloging-in-Publication Data
Names: Barnett, Brooke, 1972- editor. |
Felten, Peter, editor. Title: Intersectionality in action : a guide for
faculty and campus leaders for creating inclusive classrooms / edited
by Brooke Barnett and Peter Felten ; foreword by Eboo Patel.
Description: First edition. |
Sterling, Virginia : Stylus Publishing, LLC, 2016. |
Includes index.
Identifiers: LCCN 2015027655|
    ISBN 9781620363201 (pbk. : alk. paper) |
    ISBN 9781620363195 (cloth : alk. paper) |
    ISBN 9781620363218 (library networkable e-edition) |
    ISBN 9781620363225 (consumer e-edition)
Subjects: LCSH: Inclusive education--United States. |
Education, Higher--United States. |
Educational leadership--United States.
Classification: LCC LC1201 .I56 2015 |
DDC 371.9/046--dc23 LC record available at
http://lccn.loc.gov/2015027655
13-digit ISBN: 978-1-62036-319-5 (cloth)
13-digit ISBN: 978-1-62036-320-1 (paperback)
13-digit ISBN: 978-1-62036-321-8 (library networkable e-edition)
13-digit ISBN: 978-1-62036-322-5 (consumer e-edition)

Printed in the United States of America

All first editions printed on acid-free paper
that meets the American National Standards Institute
Z39-48 Standard.

Bulk Purchases

Quantity discounts are available for use in workshops and for
staff development.
Call 1-800-232-0223

First Edition, 2016

10   9   8   7   6   5   4   3   2

Brooke: For my parents and siblings, who supported my inclusion work long before it was a job, and for Tom, Lily, and Jack, who support it today.

Peter: For my mother, who always held my hand at the intersections.

The editors wish to thank Laura St. Cyr of Elon University for using her exceptional organizational and editorial skills to support this project.

CONTENTS

FOREWORD

In early 2015, I was invited to give a series of talks on diversity at the University of California–Los Angeles (UCLA), where I first heard the story of Rachel Beyda. Like all students, Rachel Bedya had many identities—a woman, a second-year student, an economics major, a leader in several Jewish organizations, and a 20-year-old who dreamed of a law career.

Beyda's professional aspirations led her to apply for a seat on UCLA's prestigious Judicial Board. The application process involved an interview with representatives of the UCLA student government, and the interview itself involved a set of discussions on Beyda's various identities. Interestingly, the focus of the interview had little to do with Beyda's academic major and career goals, but focused heavily on her gender and religion. Furthermore, those two identities were treated very differently. Being a woman was viewed approvingly; the student-government representatives conducting the interview argued that the Judicial Board needed more strong women. But Beyda's Jewish faith was regarded with suspicion. She was asked to respond to questions like "Given that you are a Jewish student and very active in the Jewish community, how do you see yourself being able to maintain an unbiased view?"

Beyda was then asked to leave the room so the student government could debate the issue in private. During the next 40 minutes of discussion, captured both on video and in written minutes, the student representatives decided that Beyda's Jewish identity would in fact bias her in inappropriate ways, and they voted to reject her nomination. It was not until a faculty adviser pointed out the potential prejudice at play in viewing Jewish identity as a negative mark that the students revisited the issue and ultimately approved a seat for Beyda. A few weeks later, the Beyda incident was on the front page of the *New York Times* (Nagourney, 2015) and became the most e-mailed story of that day.

The Beyda case is instructive for anyone on a college campus seeking to understand and engage the variety of identities students bring to campus. First, identity matters. Or, more accurately, identities matter—often in surprising ways. The student government representatives conducting the interview did not focus primarily on how Rachel's coursework or leadership experience prepared her for the responsibilities of serving on the Judicial Board; rather, they wanted to discuss how her gender and religion might add to or detract from the manner in which she would carry out her responsibilities. It is easy to imagine similar conversations happening around race, nationality, geography, and/or sexuality. This, of course, is a central dynamic of intersectionality theory—none of us can be reduced to a single identity, and the most salient identities in any given situation can be surprising.

It is interesting to note how gender played positively in this scenario and religion played negatively. It is hard to read this particular situation as anything other than prejudicial toward religious identity, perhaps even tinged with anti-Semitism. After all, why should the narratives, symbols, and solidarities associated with being a woman be understood positively, while the narratives, symbols, and solidarities associated with being Jewish mark someone as unfairly biased?

In lifting up intersectionality, campus professionals have an opportunity to reflect on dimensions of identity they are more comfortable working with and on those with which they feel less comfortable engaging. After all, we all bring a variety of identities to the table, identities that interact with our students' hybridity in ways that might confer privilege upon certain identities and ignore or marginalize others.

It is also useful to pay attention to how charged the issue became. Approving a student to a leadership post on a campus happens tens of thousands of times a year, but when the process involves questions about certain dimensions of identity, the case can easily emerge as a front-page news story. One reason for the national scrutiny given to this story is that the issues at play are electric in the broader culture. National debates on gender issues, such as the dearth of women in positions of corporate leadership and the unequal pay given to men and women in similar professional roles, might well have played a part in the discussion of Beyda's femaleness as an asset. Similarly, the raging controversy over Middle East policy, and the polarization this has caused between Muslim and Jewish students on campuses, very likely played a role in the questions regarding Beyda's Jewishness. These religious and political tensions were certainly present at UCLA, where the student government had recently passed a resolution urging divestment from Israeli companies.

All of this can be boiled down to some insights that appear common-sensical while also being intensely complicated. All of us have a variety of identities. Those identities matter, guiding patterns of belief, behavior, and belonging. Identities do not exist in vacuums but are made more or less salient given larger contexts (policy debates, social movements, etc.). Different identities can lead to tension and conflict, most certainly within a diverse student body, but also within a single individual. Walt Whitman (1892) expresses this beautifully in his famous verse:

> Do I contradict myself?
> Very well then I contradict myself,
> (I am large, I contain multitudes).

I love that this line can be read as both celebrating the joys of variety and being resigned to the inevitable tensions caused by diversity.

If the primary business of campuses was to make furniture or cars, all of this might be viewed as an unwelcome distraction. But since our primary purpose is to fashion leaders for a diverse democracy, nurturing graduates who can engage these inevitable tensions in positive and proactive ways is essential to the work of a college campus.

This work—as we all know—can range from difficult and frustrating one day to inspiring and heartwarming the next. The good news is that you hold in your hands a book that raises the right questions and casts light upon possible answers for shaping campus communities that serve as both laboratories for our diverse democracy and launching pads for a new generation of leaders. May it enrich our work, our campuses, our students, and our shared future.

Eboo Patel
Founder and President
Interfaith Youth Core
Chicago, Illinois

References

Nagourney, A. (2015, March 5). In U.C.L.A. debate over Jewish student, echoes on campus of old biases. *New York Times*. Retrieved from http://www.nytimes.com/2015/03/06/us/debate-on-a-jewish-student-at-ucla.html?_r=0

Whitman, W. (1892). *Song of myself*. Retrieved from http://www.poetryfoundation.org/poem/174745

INTRODUCTION

Working at the Intersections

Brooke Barnett and Peter Felten

Issues of diversity and inclusion are central in higher education today, and they will only become more important in the future as U.S. demographics change and globalization accelerates. Many colleges and universities have developed elaborate programs and structures to support inclusive excellence. Nearly every campus has academic departments that study and teach human diversity, student life programs that welcome and support people with a range of identities, and human resource specialists to train faculty and staff in best (and in legal) practices.

However, the people on our campuses—the students, faculty, and staff—do not encounter diversity in the fractured ways that match the organizational structures of our institutions. For instance, a student is not an accounting major in the classroom, a woman in her living-learning community, a first-generation college student in her advising support group, and a visa-holding undergraduate when working with administrators on paperwork in preparation for a semester abroad. Instead, she is all of those things at once. Additionally, an individual's identity is not fixed; it evolves over time, and different aspects of identity might be more or less salient in different contexts. Still, as Ruthellen Josselson (1996) explained in her book *Revising Herself*, we typically do not experience the world from the perspective of only one facet of our identity, but see ourselves as an integrated whole: "Living our identities is much like breathing. We don't have to ask ourselves each morning who we are. We simply are" (p. 29). *good point*

That unity is rarely supported on campus. Most higher education institutions are structured in ways that make organizational sense but may not reflect the experiences and needs of our students. For example, a report published by the American Council on Education (ACE) critiqued the ubiquitous division between international and multicultural education programs on campuses across the United States (Olson, Evans, & Schoenberg, 2007). Students learn about diverse people and cultures, and about themselves, in remarkably similar ways through these two parallel structures. Almost a decade ago, the ACE suggested that this division should be bridged, if not eliminated. Since that ACE report appeared, however, few institutions have adopted its recommendations; many programs, even excellent ones, operate within organizational silos. international v. Diversity

We believe that the time has come for institutions to move intentionally toward intersections—of study abroad and multiculturalism, of race and gender and religion, and of other essential aspects of our educational programs and our students' identities.

This will not be easy. Exploring the intersections is complex work that can create new (or exacerbate existing) social or political tensions, and it may prompt competition for scarce resources. However, a focus on intersections opens doors to new possibilities that better prepare our students for life in a diverse world. It also allows our institutions to become more efficient and effective as we strive not simply to do things better in our own separate spheres, but to do better things by working together across difference.

To encourage such a shift, Sturm (2006) emphasized the need for "institutional mindfulness" to ensure that we are attending to the complexity of inclusion work on a college campus. This requires "creating institutional roles that place people with knowledge, influence, and credibility in positions to influence practice at pivotal locations" within an organization and a community (Sturm, 2006, p. 251). While being positioned at the institutional intersections is essential, it is not enough. We also need attentiveness to the plural, fluid, and intersecting identities of individuals on our campuses (students, faculty, staff, and others). Only by attending to all of these intersections will we ensure that both diversity across the university and diversity within and among groups are at the center of higher education.

This book aims to help readers, no matter what position they occupy on campus, to develop the knowledge and capacities necessary to do this essential work.

Throughout this book, chapter authors use intersectionality as a framework to examine how a particular topic affects individuals, groups, policies, and programs on campus. Intersectionality is rooted in the premise that understanding identity, oppression, power, and marginalization cannot be accomplished by looking solely at single identities. This is not an entirely new idea. In the 1850s, for instance, Sojourner Truth asked, "Ain't I a woman?" and challenged the reformers at a women's convention to consider how gender and race intersect in American society (Painter, 1997). More than a century later, law professor Kimberlé Crenshaw (1989) coined the term suggested by Truth—*intersectionality*. Crenshaw used this framework to explain that various biological, social, and cultural identities interact dynamically and must be critically examined to fully understand the basis of discrimination or oppression.

Researchers and educators now use intersectionality to go beyond a single aspect of identity or inequality and analyze how multiple aspects of identities and inequalities factor into experiences with power, inequality, and difference (Dill, McLaughlin, & Nieves, 2007). Intersectionality, in short, "provides a critical analytic lens to interrogate racial, ethnic, class, physical ability, age, sexuality, and gender disparities and to contest existing ways of looking at these structures of inequality" (Dill & Zambrana, 2009, p. 1).

Weber (1998) argued that prior to this emphasis on intersectionality, scholarship generally treated *identity* as "assigned a single location along a dimension, which is defined by a set of presumably mutually exclusive and exhaustive categories" (p. 18). This approach was and still is helpful for research and practice focused on single aspects of identity. The "single story" framework provides the basis of much of what we know, for example, about racial identity formation, and higher education researchers and practitioners commonly disaggregate data into distinct categories as a useful practice to ensure that variances across groups are understood. Yet such single-identity data rarely address the differences within groups or the impact of intersecting identities on students' experiences in higher education (Bowleg, 2008; Jones & Abes, 2013; Jones & McEwen, 2000). Although intersectionality can provide a clarifying lens to focus on the complexities of diversity on campus, it is not without flaws; perhaps most importantly, some scholars have cautioned that attention to intersectionality in higher education can unintentionally obscure real differences by "flattening," or inappropriately equating all aspects of identity (Luft, 2009 p. 104).

While the perils of superficial analysis are real, we believe that the intersectional framework provides a helpful heuristic for exploring questions of diversity and inclusion in colleges and universities (Mitchell, Simmons, & Greyerbiehl, 2014; Ouellett, 2011). Like any heuristic, it is not perfect. However, focusing on the intersections helps us to be attentive to both the complexity of individual experiences on campus and the organizational structures that make it possible (or seemingly impossible) for us to engage deeply with difficult questions of diversity and inclusion.

This book explores the practices and perspectives necessary for rethinking higher education to focus on the intersections of identity. Building on the emerging literature about intersectionality and on the rich scholarship about diversity and inclusion and rooted in the context of a range of different campuses, this book includes chapters by an array of experts from different institutions and roles. Each chapter offers action-oriented analysis focusing on particular campus intersections, rather than attending to specific demographic groups. Chapter authors also build on their own local expertise of doing this work on campuses that often do not have deep pockets or rich histories of such efforts.

The book is organized into three parts:

✓ 1. **People** focuses on the broad concept of diversity, considering how we recruit and engage the students, faculty, and staff in the campus community and how we work with governing boards and others to promote inclusive excellence.

✓ 2. **Environment** focuses on inclusion, including residence life, the local community, the working and learning environment, and external factors, such as national and international news events or town-gown relationships.

✓ 3. **Learning** focuses on perspective taking and learning about difference in the core curriculum, the disciplines, and the cocurriculum, as well as professional development for faculty and staff.

Part One: People

Chapter 1: *Student Recruitment and Retention at the Intersections: A Case for Capacity Building by Alta Mauro and Angela Mazaris*

This chapter explores innovative approaches to recruitment and retention of students, supporting identity without silos. It focuses on student identity formation and development and explores ways to ensure that an institution's strategy attends to the needs of current and future students while also navigating the legal and practical complexities of this work.

Chapter 2: *Recruitment and Retention at the Intersections: Colleagues by Paul Parsons*

This chapter considers maintaining staff for continuity and development, creating positive personal and professional environments. While the student population turns over with every admissions and graduation cycle, faculty and staff colleagues often spend many years at an institution. How can an institution address recruitment and retention in ways that create a workplace of choice for colleagues from all backgrounds?

Chapter 3: *Leadership at the Intersection: A Developmental Framework for Inclusive Leaders by Niki Latino*

This chapter explores a developmental model, grounded in critical race theory, of White inclusive leadership. The chapter considers the implications and applications of this framework for leaders who have majority status in other salient identity categories (e.g., religion or sexuality) in their campus context.

Chapter 4: *Leaders, Governing Bodies, and Advisory Boards by Jeff Stein and Leo M. Lambert*

This chapter offers concrete examples and practical advice to engage campus boards, advisers, and institutional leaders with the important work of diversity and inclusion.

Chapter 5: *It Takes a Campus: Building Capacity to Sustain the Diversity Journey by Michael A. McDonald, Sarah B. Westfall, and Eileen B. Wilson-Oyelaran*

This chapter uses institutional and personal stories to stress the importance of personal commitment and agency for everyone on campus—faculty, staff, and administration—to further the goals of diversity and inclusion. How do we cultivate the buy-in and develop change agents across a campus (not just among the likely subjects)?

Part Two: Environment

Chapter 6: *Striving for an Inclusive and Nurturing Campus: Cultivating the Intersections by Jon Dooley and Lucy LePeau*

This chapter emphasizes the essential role of partnerships in the complex work of cultivating an inclusive campus climate for all students, faculty, and staff.

Chapter 7: *When Things Go Wrong: Avoiding and Managing Collisions in the Intersections by Leigh-Anne Royster*

This chapter focuses on creating and implementing bias and discrimination response and education teams that can function effectively across a range of identity and programmatic intersections.

Chapter 8: *Bringing Life to Learning: Civic Engagement, Intersections, and Transforming College Students by Amy Howard, Juliette Landphair, and Amanda Lineberry*

This chapter considers the location of the university, acknowledging it as both an asset and a challenge. How do you effectively cultivate the diverse assets within your local community, creating complementary intersections between town and gown?

Part Three: Learning

Chapter 9: *Diversifying Diversity, Diversifying Disability by Danielle R. Picard and Nancy L. Chick*

This chapter considers how ability and disability intersect in classrooms and shape the learning experience for all students.

Chapter 10: *Leadership for a Global Caring Society by Ed Taylor*

This chapter uses a single undergraduate course as a case study to explore how the diverse identities and experiences students bring to a classroom can prompt critical reflection on the larger purposes and practices of higher education.

Chapter 11: *The Intersection of Life and Learning: What Cultural Wealth and Liberal Education Mean for Whole Student Development by Ashley Finley and Tia McNair*

This chapter considers how the process of learning is central to students' personal and civic identity formation.

Conclusion: *Guiding Principles for Working at the Intersections by Brooke Barnett and Peter Felten*

This final section synthesizes the essential principles and practices from the previous chapters while emphasizing the need for thoughtful assessment and strategic planning to put intersectionality into action in all aspects of the university.

The practices and scholarship in these chapters capture some of the power of using intersectionality to think about and organize diversity and inclusion work on campus. Moving from theory to practice is rarely easy, but it is fundamental to the mission and purpose of higher education.

References

Bowleg, L. (2008). When Black + lesbian + woman ≠ Black lesbian woman: The methodological challenges of qualitative and quantitative intersectionality research. *Sex Roles, 59*, 312–325.

Crenshaw, K. (1989). Demarginalizing the intersection of race and sex: A Black feminist critique of antidiscrimination doctrine, feminist theory and antiracist politics. *University of Chicago legal forum, feminism in the law: Theory, practice and criticism,* vol. 1989 (139–167). Chicago, IL: University of Chicago Legal Forum.

Dill, B. T., McLaughlin, A. E., & Nieves, A. D. (2007). Future directions of feminist research: Intersectionality. In S. N. Hesse-Biber (Ed.), *Handbook of feminist research* (pp. 629–637). Thousand Oaks, CA: Sage.

Dill, B. T., & Zambrana, R. E. (2009). *Emerging intersections: Race, class, and gender in theory, policy, and practice.* New Brunswick, NJ: Rutgers University Press.

Jones, S. R. (1997). Voices of identity and difference: A qualitative exploration of the multiple dimensions of identity development in women college students. *Journal of College Student Development, 38,* 376–386.

Jones, S. R., & Abes, E. S. (2013). *Identity development of college students: Advancing frameworks for multiple dimensions of identity.* San Francisco, CA: Jossey-Bass.

Jones, S. R., & McEwen, M. K. (2000). A conceptual model of multiple dimensions of identity. *Journal of College Student Development, 41,* 405–414.

Josselson, R. E. (1996). *Revising herself: The story of women's identity from college to midlife.* New York, NY: Oxford University Press.

Luft, R. E. (2009). Intersectionality and the risk of flattening difference: Gender and race logics, and the strategic use of antiracist singularity. In M. T. Berg & K. Guidroz (Eds.), *The intersectional approach: Transforming the academy through race, class, and gender* (pp. 100–117). Chapel Hill: University of North Carolina Press.

Mitchell, D., Jr., Simmons, C. Y., & Greyerbiehl, L. A. (Eds.). (2014). *Intersectionality and higher education: Theory, research, and praxis.* New York, NY: Peter Lang.

Olson, C. L., Evans, R., & Schoenberg, R. E. (2007). *At home in the world: Bridging the gap between internationalization and multicultural education.* Washington, DC: American Council on Education.

Ouellett, M. L. (Ed.). (2011). *An integrative analysis approach to diversity in the college classroom.* New directions for teaching and learning #125. San Francisco, CA: Jossey-Bass.

Painter, N. I. (1997). *Sojourner Truth: A life, a symbol.* New York, NY: W. W. Norton.

Sturm, S. P. (2006). The architecture of inclusion: Advancing workplace equity in higher education. *Harvard Journal of Law & Gender, 29*(2), 247–334. Retrieved from http://ssrn.com/abstract=901992

Weber, L. (1998). A conceptual framework for understanding race, class, gender, and sexuality. *Psychology of Women Quarterly, 22,* 13–22.

PART ONE

PEOPLE

I

STUDENT RECRUITMENT AND RETENTION AT THE INTERSECTIONS

A Case for Capacity Building

Alta Mauro and Angela Mazaris

Conventional wisdom around the recruitment and retention of diverse students is founded on several assumptions:

- *Diversity* is traditionally defined solely as students of color.
- Success is measured by the number of students of color who enroll each year.
- Responsibility for recruiting and retaining diverse students lies primarily with multicultural centers and offices of diversity and inclusion, and sometimes with women's centers and lesbian, gay, bisexual, transgender, and queer (LGBTQ) centers.

This chapter seeks to reframe the conversation around student recruitment and retention by focusing on institutional capacity building. We posit an institution-wide integrative model that acknowledges the many different identities of our students. By breaking down silos between departments and units, this approach strategically empowers divisions, departments, and offices throughout the institution to approach the day-to-day work of diversity and inclusion as part of their core organizational mission.

The capacity-building model proposes an alternative framework for thinking about recruitment and retention. Tenets of this approach include the following:

- The term *diversity* refers to a broad mix of potential identities, including race, ethnicity, nationality, religion, age, socioeconomic status, gender, sexual orientation, gender identity and expression, and disability, as well as differences in life experiences, intellectual background, and political viewpoint.

- Students from underrepresented groups often need specific forms of support, as not all identity categories shape student experiences in the same way.
- Successful recruitment and retention of a diverse mix of students require broad-based cultural competence across institutional structures, including within offices, departments, and divisions that are not explicitly charged with "doing diversity."
- Our model of capacity building is specifically focused on building this cultural competence capacity in a range of spaces, including but not limited to academic departments, admissions offices, financial aid offices, and student affairs divisions.

In this chapter we present a rationale for embracing the capacity-building model as a best practice for the recruitment and retention of students traditionally defined as *diverse*. We also point to specific examples of how institutions have incorporated aspects of this model into their policies and practices. We hope this chapter will serve as a resource for institutions seeking innovative and cross-cutting strategies for diversity recruitment and retention.

We define *capacity building* in this context as a system in which staff and faculty competence around diversity and inclusion is considered a core institutional value and a key indicator of success across departments and disciplines. Within a capacity-building model, staff diversity and inclusion competencies are regularly assessed, implemented or improved, and reassessed. Diversity and inclusion are explicitly articulated as values and are inextricably linked to the university's mission. Efforts to expand institutional capacity typically include training, coaching, and mentoring. These efforts are measured as part of performance goals at the individual, departmental, and institutional level. Embedded in strategic planning cycles, a commitment to continual investment in professional development at this level has the potential for systemic, sustainable, and measurable impact.

Shifts in Support: Affirmative Action, Multiculturalism, and Inclusion

Throughout the second half of the twentieth century, numerous shifts have occurred in the provisions made for women, people of color, and other historically marginalized or underserved populations in higher education. Perhaps the most notable public policy is affirmative action, which emerged from the civil rights movement of the 1960s as a method of ensuring equal opportunities for women and members of minority groups in both education and employment. Universities adopted the policy upon President Lyndon Johnson's 1965 executive order, after which African American and Latino college enrollment began to increase steadily ("Affirmative Action," n.d.).

As critical masses of students of color began matriculating, universities moved to establish formal support and resources for underrepresented minority groups, primarily through offices of minority affairs. The role of such centers ranged from supporting efforts to recruit (mostly) Black students to providing safe and affirming spaces for those experiencing university life at the margins, both of which correlated to greater minority student retention. As enrollment of other ethnic minorities and international students increased, many staff and students called for an expansion of support services beyond those for Black students. In developing offices of multicultural affairs and/or cultural centers, university officials linked strategies for improved campus climate to specific administrative offices (Patton, 2012). While this anchoring provided direct points of contact and support for students of color, it situated accountability for them and the campus issues that were indicative of increasing structural diversity with the staff and faculty in those spaces. In short, the community work of achieving excellence in diversity was, in many cases, systematically siloed among a very few professionals. Administrative offices designed to offer support for LGBTQ student communities have been similarly siloed.

Positioning such rich resources within these narrow confines leaves administrators overburdened if they attempt to do such critical work alone. Additionally, these models limit the opportunities of colleagues in other functional areas to develop skills that support our most vulnerable students. While traditional understandings of diversity have focused on race and ethnicity as defining factors of identity, today's students often consider themselves members of multiple identity groups. For example, a Black student may be aware of not only her racial identity but also her identity as a lesbian and first-generation college student. Particular attention must be paid to the experiences students bring to campus and the intersectionality of their identities in order to craft support systems that meet their varied needs. This shift from isolated support of specific demographic groups to a more integrated approach to inclusion is a critical adjustment that many universities have made in efforts to push beyond historically raced language and related tensions. Often, this shift results in the establishment of an office of equity, diversity, and inclusion. Such a unit is typically headed by a chief

help us work together

diversity officer who reports directly to the president. When appropriately established and utilized, such an office can provide institutional leadership around diversity and inclusion from an intersectional lens and help colleagues throughout the university to appreciate, engage, and practice empathy across lines of nationality, religion, ethnicity, race, class, gender, sexual orientation, and social location.

equality to equity

The focus on both structural diversity and inclusive practice elevates our approach to student support from one focused on *equality* (i.e., equal representation vis-à-vis admissions and retention numbers) to an approach designed to achieve *equity*. This is a fundamental paradigm shift, in that efforts to maintain equality ignore social stratification, which relegates non-dominant groups to subordinate positions on the margins. Equity, however, acknowledges unequal access to full participation in the campus community, thus seeking acknowledgment and redress of historical barriers and creating opportunities for historically underserved groups to engage in meaningful and culturally relevant ways.

✻

Despite the viability of cultural centers and the additional reach of the diversity and inclusion paradigm, universities must take further steps to adequately recruit and retain diverse students. One method of bolstering such support is the adoption of a capacity-building model.

Moving Beyond Silos in Recruitment and Engagement

In many institutions, responsibilities for recruitment lie solely with admissions teams, largely unaffected by colleagues in offices of diversity and inclusion, multicultural centers, or other functional areas. Whereas it makes sense that staff in admissions work alone in estimating yield and other, more calculated aspects of the process, it is critical that a cross section of stakeholders work collaboratively to influence conversations about prospective student readiness and "institutional fit." The latter concept may be the most critical, as "institutional fit" is often the language used to describe students whose identities do not match the majority of the student body, or whose cultural values require them to engage in behaviors that are sometimes foreign to those in the majority. It is not uncommon for staff and faculty who are engaged in efforts to support historically underserved students to be critical of admissions offices, the seemingly shrouded nature of their processes, and what appears to be ambivalence toward calls for greater student diversity. When silos are broken down, however, and colleagues are invited to work in partnership with admissions officers, they can develop greater appreciation for the complexity involved in recruiting and admitting a class. These advocates may also educate admissions staff on critical histories that affect student identity and the barriers prospective students may perceive between themselves and the university. This deeper understanding engenders wider institutional ownership over the recruitment-to-retention cycle, and it positions colleagues to commit to more genuine support of university efforts in this regard.

Beyond facilitating greater institutional commitment to admissions work, this approach deepens the capacity of those working in admissions. As they expose their workflow and invite critique, they are able to devise new strategies for success through the lens of colleagues working across functional areas. Over time, the admissions officer who leaned on staff in an LGBTQ center to engage openly gay students comes to see herself as capable of responding to student need appropriately as a result of her sustained engagement with colleagues in that area. That same admissions officer may have had initial reservations about supporting a growing, ethnically diverse Muslim student population. As a result of her exposure to identity development theories and the concept of intersectionality, the officer may be better equipped to engage these students and their families in authentic dialogue about their needs or reservations, as opposed to simply suggesting that the student connect with staff in the chaplain's office. Similarly, partnering with faculty in history, sociology, or economics to educate financial aid staff on the complex history of class and access to wealth capitalizes on the university's intellectual command and boosts the capacity of financial aid offices to offer nuanced approaches to student need.

Just as a siloed understanding of identity limits us from admitting increasingly diverse cohorts and fully understanding their needs, a siloed approach to diversity and inclusion prevents us from meeting those needs adequately. For example, consider the student affairs professional who directs a university cultural center, supervising a small staff. Colleagues value the work the director has organized through the center, and they routinely call upon the director for support in ensuring that their own work is sensitive and culturally relevant. In any given year, this individual can accurately report that between 20% and 30% of his or her time spent at work is dedicated to researching, troubleshooting, and otherwise negotiating sensitive cultural issues with—and often for—colleagues who lack cultural competence skills or who do not believe in their abilities to navigate such terrain more independently. For many middle managers, this translates to almost a full work day per week spent in significant operation in different functional areas. Imagine that same director being free to use that time to advance his or her departmental mission. A capacity-building model creates opportunities for the director to train or coach professional peers on cultural competence and culturally relevant pedagogy, empowering them to act more independently.

Rather than serving as a proxy employee in multiple functional areas, the director can operate as a consultant to colleagues, advising to a degree, but not becoming enmeshed in others' work.

In short, we should approach staff and faculty competence with the same high expectations we apply to other aspects of our work and provide support for the continual development of other competencies, with a challenge to achieve excellence.

Capacity Building in Action

Effective capacity building toward increased student engagement and retention requires assessing the breadth and depth of current efforts and understanding which schools, units, or departments are working intentionally toward the university's equity goals. For example, in an attempt to determine the range of cultural/intercultural efforts already in place, New York University–Abu Dhabi staff have launched a heat-mapping project, in which staff and faculty across the university are asked to indicate how their work has encouraged student self-awareness related to culture, intercultural communication, or intercultural understanding. At the time of publication, student affairs staff were being asked to participate in focus groups by functional area in order to determine the degree to which their work addresses these topics, and to find ways to maximize the impact of these efforts. Initiated by the newly launched Office of Intercultural Education and Spiritual Life, this surveying method has revealed great opportunities for intentional collaboration to deliver more of what Kuh calls "high-impact educational practices" (Kuh, 2008, p. 21).

The key project deliverable is a heat map, which will depict the colleges, programs, and departments where intercultural efforts must be undertaken consciously versus those where the nature of the academic discipline necessitates the consideration of culture, globalization, and so forth (e.g., in political science departments or study abroad programs). An analysis of the map may reveal the institutional structures or practices that interact to reinforce either equity or bias. The heat map will also depict whether there are colleges, programs, and departments where there are no relevant efforts in place. Critically, this map could reveal that there are physical spaces on campus that are devoid of intercultural efforts, or that are otherwise a chilly climate for diverse students where microaggressions are common and psychological damage related to "-isms" is likely to occur (Sedlacek & Brooks, 1976). Armed with the information that there are certain stretches of campus where efforts toward intercultural education and equity are challenged, administrators can strategize an appropriate institutional response. A commitment to continual campus audit work of this kind positions senior leaders to focus energy and resources on boosting capacity in the least effective areas.

While we offer capacity building as a model for structural integration of student support, we recognize that many of us face challenges within our institutions because of structural silos, scarcity of resources, and student engagement. Here, we offer examples of institutions that have sought creative solutions to the challenges of recruiting and retaining a diverse student body.

Structural Barriers

There are numerous structural barriers to effective student recruitment and retention. First, from a social and economic perspective, we recognize that many students face structural challenges that are larger than our educational institutions. Colleges and universities must grapple with the disparate impacts of race and socioeconomic status on their students, and the ways in which these and other identities impact both who applies to college and how they fare when they matriculate. Second, we recognize that within universities themselves, organizational structures may hamper attempts at providing integrated support throughout the recruitment and retention process.

The University of Texas at Austin (UT Austin) has adopted promising practices to lower some of these barriers. Faculty and administrators have used data from the Office of Institutional Research to create the UT System Dashboard to predict student success. By calibrating a number of factors that include SAT scores, high school class rank, family income, and first-generation status, the Dashboard identifies those students at the greatest risk of not completing their degrees on time. Officials have used these data to create targeted supports, including smaller classes, additional mentorship and guidance, and leadership development programs aimed at raising both academic and professional success (Tough, 2014; see also www.utsystem.edu/offices/strategic-initiatives/productivity-dashboard).

Researchers at Stanford University, UT Austin, and elsewhere have also shown that offering at-risk students basic, positive messages about ability and belonging can significantly improve their chances of success. When students in a nondominant group (students of color, women, first-generation students, etc.) hear messages related to the following themes early in their academic career, they are statistically more likely to achieve results on par with their peers from dominant groups:

- Belonging: Students from at-risk and nondominant groups often feel a profound sense of social and academic nonbelonging when they arrive on campus. Simple messaging stating that it is normal to feel this way and that it is a temporary state helps prevent students from becoming alienated and derailed by this sense of difference.

- Ability: At-risk students who experience failure early in their college careers (e.g., a poor test grade, a lower GPA than expected) often internalize this failure and consider it evidence of their lack of suitability for higher education. Early messaging to students that failure is a normal part of learning and that brains are malleable—and thus capable of growth and expansion—gives students the confidence to keep trying after early setbacks.

While these interventions should not be seen as magic bullets—they certainly do not undo the discrepancies in preparation and resources that exist between various groups of students—they have consistently been shown to positively impact student performance (Walton & Cohen, 2011; Yeager & Dweck, 2012). In a pilot experiment conducted at UT Austin, all incoming first-year students were exposed to one of four messages: a message that targeted either belonging, ability, belonging and ability, or a random control message. The at-risk students who received the combined messaging about belonging and ability were significantly more likely to complete at least 12 credits of coursework in their first semester than their at-risk peers who watched the control message (Tough, 2014).

While not all colleges and universities have the capacity to develop a sophisticated data tracking system like the UT System Dashboard, incorporating messaging to all incoming students about belonging and ability is a way to overcome some perceived barriers. At Wake Forest University, for example, as part of their training, all lower-division academic advisers are instructed to provide this messaging to their new advisees in group and individual advising sessions. This ensures that those students potentially at risk of noncompletion, regardless of whether they are identified early, receive these messages in their first days of university life.

Staffing, Resources, and Silos

As we have noted, a move toward a capacity-building model of diversity recruitment and retention requires working across silos to ensure that offices, departments, and divisions across the university are equipped to support a diverse range of students as part of their core mission. Using a capacity-building approach can also provide institutions with opportunities to strategically deploy resources for maximum impact.

One method of increasing staff capacity to support inclusive excellence is a quarter-time, or collateral duty, system, in which employees in one functional area are allowed to work on specific projects in another area for roughly a quarter of their weekly working hours. Lehigh University maximizes this system among entry-level staff who have expressed interest in learning about various functional areas under the dean of students umbrella. These new professionals not only add competencies to their repertoire, but also become pseudo- or proxy staff in what are typically understaffed departments. A small student affairs division could benefit from this form of cross-training while investing in its team's development. Further, a rotating system allows for a continual newness that encourages employee engagement. In short, the opportunity to work a quarter-time position may lead to greater staff development, engagement, and retention, as well as create increased support for at-risk students. Bates College employs a different spin on job sharing with their "Swing Dean" program, in which two staff members share two traditionally separate roles, one in the admissions office and one in the dean of students' office. Rather than having a diversity dean for admissions who helps to recruit students and a different diversity dean within the student affairs division who supports students once they matriculate, Bates has combined these two positions into a two-year rotating job, held by two staff members. Each dean spends one year recruiting a new class of students (with a particular focus on students of color and first-generation college students), *cool* and then moves into the dean of students' office to serve as that group's class dean for freshman year. The Bates program builds on the close relationships underrepresented students often form with the admissions representatives who recruit them and leverages those relationships to provide the kind of support that bolsters student retention—without creating new full-time positions.

As these examples demonstrate, developing diversity and inclusion competence for staff in units across the university has a twofold value. First, it supports the institutional goals of recruiting and retaining a diverse student body, and second, it bolsters the missions of individual units across the campus by providing added value to their core functions.

Student Engagement and Intersectionality

Supporting college students can be immensely rewarding work. It is especially gratifying to witness students coming to identify who they are—and who they will be—in the world. Practitioners committed to being what Baxter-Magolda called "good company" take a special pride in mentoring *yes* young adults through identity formation (Baxter-Magolda, 2002, p. 3). The formative time from 18 to 23 years of age is typically marked by movement toward a more solidified identity, with most students consciously considering the ideological positions with which they will be aligned for the first time in their lives (Shaffer, 2005). As Shaffer noted, Erikson referred to identity formation as a "crisis," arguing that the process to find oneself has the potential to induce great stress (p. 191).

The process of learning (or claiming) one's identity becomes more complicated when students realize that a single identity does not adequately encompass their sense of self. In many cases, when people determine that they identify with more than a single identity, the already complex path to personhood becomes a winding road. Our efforts to create and maintain spaces where today's college student feels affirmed must reflect an acknowledgment of these intersections.

Interdepartmental collaborations can provide necessary linkages between support services as students come to recognize the impact of their intersecting identities. For example, staff in Wake Forest University's Office of Multicultural Affairs and Office of Sustainability collaborated to present "My Neighborhood Is Killing Me," a program focusing on environmental racism overwhelmingly affecting impoverished minority communities across the United States. In connecting issues of race, class, and systemic injustice, colleagues encouraged students from different racial minority groups to see connections between their experiences as people of color. Perhaps most critically, many students from low-resourced communities expressed that their experiences as people who are poor positioned them to have more in common with other people who are poor—despite race or ethnicity—than with middle-class or wealthy people of the same race. This linkage may seem intuitive to some, but many have not considered that there are fundamental similarities between the ways in which they and others who don't appear to be similar experience life. The organizers' goal was not to minimize the differences in their lived experiences, but to begin to establish understanding, empathy, and, ideally, coalition building across these lines of difference.

Leadership From the Top

Facilitating holistic student identity development requires integrated ideological and structural approaches, the most foundational being a shared value of inclusion at the board and cabinet levels. Trustees must understand that maintaining relevance in higher education means not only attracting a diverse student body but also ensuring that students feel safe embracing and performing the complexity of their identities. More so than structural diversity, it is students living as their authentic selves, presenting multiple perspectives and influencing each other, that actually delivers a rich learning environment.

Practitioners can add value by positioning this rationale as the business case for maintaining progressive models of inclusion. Despite genuine commitment to the academic mission of the university, trustees and senior leaders may not always understand the correlation between diversity, inclusive excellence, and the retention of top talent from a wide array of backgrounds. Armed with data from across academic and administrative units, a wise practitioner can demonstrate linkages in staff and faculty diversity, recruitment efforts and targets, curricular offerings and cycles of curricular innovation, attrition among at-risk populations, and other critical points of concern. In return, trustees can reflect a sophisticated understanding by demanding that diversity and inclusion remain top university priorities, empowering administrators to prioritize relevant action at every level of the university.

Conclusion: Capacity Building as a Best Practice

Recruitment and retention of the historically underserved in higher education are subjects of considerable public debate. As university officials consider strategic directions, it is important to reflect on both the history of these groups and current college-going trends. Further, it is essential to honor what decades of research on identity have taught us while also acknowledging the shifting notions of personhood and identity politics that mark our current social reality. It is important to include room for considerations of race, nationality, class, gender, gender expression, and sexual orientation, as well as of religious and political affiliation, in our broad definitions of *at risk*. Considering the richness that students from these groups bring to our campuses is essential, as opposed to viewing them from the oft-adopted deficit perspective. Our approach to recruiting, engaging, and supporting college students must reflect our awareness of barriers to success as well as an institutional commitment to collaborative solution building. If we are to craft new ways of achieving sustainable progress, we must think creatively about opportunities to lower the walls that separate administrative functional areas and bridge the gulfs between staff and faculty colleagues. We thus suggest a capacity-building approach, whereby ownership of university goals and responsibility toward underserved students become shared values.

References

Affirmative action. (n.d.). Retrieved from http://www.ncsl.org/research/education/affirmative-action-overview.aspx

Baxter-Magolda, M. B. (2002). Helping students make their way to adulthood: Good company for the journey. *About Campus, 6*(6), 2–9.

Kuh, G. D. (2008). *High impact educational practices: What they are, who has access to them, and why they matter.* Washington, DC: AAC&U.

Patton, L. D. (2012). *Culture centers in higher education: Perspectives on identity, theory, and practice.* Sterling, VA: Stylus.

Sedlacek, W. E., & Brooks, C. C., Jr. (1976). *Racism in American education: A model for change.* Chicago, IL: Nelson-Hall.

Shaffer, D. (2005). *Social and personality development* (5th ed.). Boston, MA: Cengage.

Tough, P. (2014, May 15) Who gets to graduate? *New York Times Magazine.* Retrieved from http://www.nytimes.com/2014/05/18/magazine/who-gets-to-graduate.html?_r=0

Walton, G., & Cohen, G. (2011). A brief social-belonging intervention improves academic and health outcomes of minority students. *Science, 331,* 1447–1451.

Yeager, D., & Dweck, C. (2012). Mindsets that promote resilience: When students believe that personal characteristics can be developed. *Educational Psychologist, 47,* 302–314.

RECRUITMENT AND RETENTION AT THE INTERSECTIONS

Colleagues

Paul Parsons

Т he student body changes with every admissions and graduation cycle, but the faculty and staff stay relatively constant. They will spend years, maybe even a career, at an institution, meaning that their selection and retention become decisions that can impact a university for decades.

The importance of a workforce mirroring the demographics of society is arguably greater for some occupations and professions than others. Diversity among those who report our news and teach our children seems more important than diversity among those who build our houses or staff an accounting firm. Diversity in the workforce is particularly important in colleges and universities, where faculty and professional staff serve as role models and mentors in guiding the education of future generations.

The value of diversity, though, sometimes encompasses words that are not really operational in a faculty or staff search. We want socioeconomic diversity, but do not explore a person's background in that way. We may value religious diversity, but do not probe into matters of faith. Ideological diversity certainly seems appropriate in an academic setting, but how would we operationalize the concept—mount a hiring spree for liberals or conservatives, depending on which is in short supply?

Diversity can be hard to achieve if you cannot see it or ask about it. As a result, diversity initiatives understandably tend to focus on gender, race, and ethnicity.

In 1900, only 4% of students in high school went on to higher education, and these elites were almost all White males (Smith & Bender, 2008).

Today, 75% of high school students spend at least some time studying in a higher education setting, and more than 35% of undergraduate students across the nation are from minority populations (U.S. Department of Education, 2013). Compare that to the National Center for Education Statistics report (U.S. Department of Education, 2014), which noted that 19% of full-time college faculty are minorities (6% Black, 4% Hispanic, 9% Asian). As Matthew Lynch (2013) put it, "More Americans from every color and creed are now earning college educations, so college faculty should reflect that. While students can certainly learn from people outside their own sex, ethnicity and belief system, faculty with similar backgrounds provide stronger role models."

Similarly, female students now outnumber male students on college campuses, yet women hold only a third of full-time professorial positions (U.S. Department of Education, 2014). These numbers are an improvement from decades before, but because faculties change more slowly than other sectors of society, these discordant numbers highlight the importance of meaningful recruitment and retention processes.

Lynch's article on the *Diverse: Issues in Higher Education* website noted the following:

> Faculty positions are extremely competitive. . . . Sometimes sex and race are simply not part of the hiring equation. Facts and figures on a resume are tangible ways to show what a particular candidate can bring to the job. It is more difficult for higher education decision makers to gauge the benefit of a person's background or life experience on the students that pay good money to learn at a particular institution. That being said, many colleges . . . try to piece together the most well-represented group of educators possible. (Lynch, 2013)

Recruiting a Diverse Faculty and Staff

Meritocracy is a good thing; candidates should be evaluated primarily on their accomplishments. But a search is nuanced. The most accomplished researcher may be a poor teacher. The candidate with the most impressive set of credentials may not be the best fit for the needs of the department. Diversity is not an end in itself, but is important as a means to an end—having a faculty and staff better mirroring the composition of students on campus because they are at the forefront of preparing the next generation.

Even before a position exists, a program can begin identifying prospective colleagues. This involves taking initiative. Some universities urge faculty and staff members to "prospect" for potential female and minority candidates at professional and academic meetings and, when vacancies occur, to recruit these individuals to the candidate pool.

Another example, sometimes used as a screening device, is to create a brown-bag luncheon series or topical panel as a way of inviting minority academics to campus. The school will benefit from their presence and guest presentations even if the faculty decide not to pursue any of the individuals as future colleagues.

For instance, a university invited a faculty member of color to be on a panel about entrepreneurship in the discipline. It went well, and she received a second invitation to campus a few months later. For the second meeting, she was scheduled to have an hour with the dean following the presentation. She wondered why. A few days before her trip, she received a revised agenda that included a tour of the city with a real estate agent at the end of the day. Very odd, she thought, because it appeared she was being recruited for a position she had not applied for. Still, why not see where this may be leading? In her meeting with the dean, she was offered an administrative position that was at the dean's discretion, and she ultimately accepted the position.

Many in the academy would find this veiled search process to be annoying, and it poses the question of whether the person may be entering an environment where the faculty were not enthusiastic about the plan. In addition, most openings are not at the discretion of an individual, but involve an appointed search committee.

The formation of a search committee is the typical way of conducting a search. The composition of search committees, of course, should be diverse. This helps mitigate the very understandable tendency for search committee members to select people like themselves to be their future colleagues. If a department does not have sufficient female or minority representation to prevent one or two colleagues from the undue burden of always being asked to serve, think about drawing on a faculty member from a related discipline who can make the committee representationally diverse and also add a fresh perspective to the search process.

Just as a course is organized through the creation of a syllabus, a faculty search needs an organizational structure. Start with the position description. The narrower the parameters, the narrower the search will be. In an age of increasing specialization, a faculty position can be constructed with such specificity that it attracts only a handful of applicants. The first step in attracting a more diverse applicant pool, then, is to craft a position description as broadly as is feasible. Larger departments have an advantage here because their faculties are large enough to provide some flexibility. Still, a mind-set must exist that having a diverse faculty is as important to the well-being of an academic program as a specialization wish list.

An institution may simply advertise a position in the *Chronicle of Higher Education* and through disciplinary organizations and, well, *hope* for a decent applicant pool. This unimaginative strategy can be ineffective if a program wants a diverse applicant pool.

Think about ways to be proactive. Spread the word among professional and academic organizations representing persons of diverse backgrounds. Send special mailings to historically Black institutions with graduate programs in the discipline. Make personal calls to friends and colleagues at other institutions.

For example, a school with a growing Hispanic student body but few Hispanic faculty decided to be proactive. Faculty members called their own PhD-granting institutions to see if they had Hispanic doctoral candidates that year. One large state university did, and the school made a special invitation to a doctoral student to be part of a candidate pool. She impressed the current faculty, was offered a position, and three years later is an outstanding colleague. Frankly, she may not have emerged as the top candidate had the school been conducting a narrow disciplinary search. But by having more freedom with respect to disciplinary focus, the university identified her as an excellent faculty member who enhances diversity while contributing to the discipline overall.

Ensure that every hiring pool contains diverse candidates before selection of finalists is made. While exceptions may need to exist for highly specialized positions that typically attract fewer applicants, the fact remains that when a hiring pool contains no women or minorities, the outcome is already predetermined in terms of gender and racial diversity.

Some search committees appoint a member to serve as a "diversity advocate" so that the committee does not lose sight of the value of a diverse candidate pool as it begins to select finalists. At this stage, a committee's focus often centers solely on credentials. Having someone at the table (ideally someone other than a minority) reminding the committee about other important considerations can be helpful. Some institutions would rather have every search committee member primed to see and value diversity in the candidate pool. The belief is that a diversity advocate might cause other members to close their eyes to diversity, relying instead on the advocate to bring forward a diverse candidate worthy of consideration.

Here, however, is where an administrator can make a difference. Sometimes a search committee has settled on its top two or three candidates based on credentials; who could argue with that? But if there is a worthy candidate in the wider pool who would add to a program's diversity, a dean could increase the number of finalists by one to ensure a campus visit by a diverse candidate. The diverse candidate may sweep the faculty off its collective feet and receive the first offer, or may emerge as an attractive candidate in the finalist pool in the event the first choice does not accept an offer.

The concept of "cluster hiring" is possible in larger university environments. The cluster hiring of faculty members in multiple departments was originally designed to expand interdisciplinary efforts, but faculty clusters also have the potential to help diversify a university's faculty and improve institutional climate. A report from the Urban Universities for Health recommended being up-front about diversity goals when cluster hiring (Urban Universities for Health, 2015).

Two alternatives to permanent faculty positions are visiting professors and adjunct faculty. Both can play an important role in adding to diversity.

For instance, a school invited an Iraqi professor to come to the United States as a visiting professor for three years. The professor was not a perfect fit in terms of discipline, but was ideal for a general education course about global experiences. Students appreciated his expertise and international perspective, colleagues learned from his vastly different professional experiences, and the university was able to make the faculty appointment permanent.

Adjunct faculty are essential in higher education these days. In fact, the American Association of University Professors reports that *adjunct faculty*, defined as full-time and part-time faculty in non-tenure-track positions, make up three-quarters of the teaching force at U.S. colleges and universities, totaling more than one million instructors (Salomon-Fernandez, 2015). Most programs do not conduct formal searches for adjunct faculty. Instead, they recruit locally for PhD holders in the discipline or working professionals, depending on the discipline. Urban universities have a huge advantage in being able to hire women and minorities as adjunct faculty. Programs in areas with fewer available part-time faculty often lament their geographic realities that limit the diversity of adjunct pools, requiring greater proactivity on their part to attract a diverse applicant pool.

Indeed, academic programs have multiple sets of goals in faculty selection: educational credentials; professional experience (in professional programs); the academic triumvirate of teaching, scholarship, and service; the ubiquitous institutional "fit"; and the need for diversity in gender, race, and ethnicity.

In their diversity plans, some schools carefully add diversity aspects to the criteria that will be considered. Here is one example: "The school will use a candidate's potential for increasing ethnic and cultural diversity in teaching perspectives, research interests and professional role models as a major criterion for recruitment, evaluation and selection." Another school refers to a candidate's racial diversity as a "non-traditional strength," further describing it as "the ability to attract minority students or offer new and different research ideas." One school includes a blunt preferential statement in its diversity plan: "All other factors being considered equal, minorities and women will be given preference over male members of the majority" (ASJMC Diversity Committee, 2008, p. 11).

Scheduling the campus visit offers another opportunity to attend to diversity. For instance, if a finalist is African American, he or she may want to visit with other African Americans on campus to gauge the community and campus environment and to ask questions in a risk-free way. A host university will show sensitivity to diverse candidates if it offers to schedule such a conversation. In fact, the best practice is to offer personalized conversation options to all candidates so that those less visible forms of diversity such as religion or sexual orientation can also be addressed. For example, this prompt may lead to questions about parental leave policies and balancing work and life with small children, or questions from single colleagues about community-building opportunities.

Sometimes finalists themselves take the initiative on a sensitive point before the campus visit. For example, a few days before a finalist made his campus visit, he sent the department chair an e-mail letting her know that, for religious reasons, he would not be shaking her hand or the hand of any female faculty or staff member during his visit. This triggered a spirited discussion among faculty about whether this was a custom to accept, or whether it might be indicative of a practice of treating women in the workplace as inferior. Upon the candidate's arrival, faculty were surprised to discover the candidate was a Minnesotan of Irish descent who had recently converted to Islam. The debate over handshaking became a moot point when his teaching and scholarly presentations went poorly. → and he was white!

Laws govern the faculty and staff search process. For example, it is illegal to ask questions regarding gender, race, ethnicity, sexual orientation, disability, and religion, to name a few factors. A search must be unbiased in regard to these factors, so it serves no useful purpose to know them. Nevertheless, the government requires state institutions to report statistics on applicant pools to the best of their ability. A number of institutions consider it less burdensome and more accurate to send personal data forms to the applicant pool rather than review each CV in an effort to determine the numbers of women and minorities in the applicant pool. In one search, for example, committee members assumed that a candidate whose research focused on African Americans and the media was African American. He was not.

Search committees at many universities operate under affirmative action policies that require a broad and inclusive search process, with institutional officers looking over the shoulders of search committees. Lists must be generated showing recruitment efforts to reach diverse populations, the diversity of the applicant pool, the diversity of those invited to interview on campus, and ultimately the one offered the position. On at least one campus, if no offer is made to a minority individual among the finalists, the affirmative action office requires a written report explaining the reason for not hiring the individual. If an offer is declined, a school may wish to conduct a follow-up interview with the diverse candidate to determine the reason, in hopes of learning something that will help the next search be more successful.

In sum, consider the following best practices in recruiting:

- Think of faculty and staff recruiting as continuous and proactive, not as periodic and occurring only when a position is available. This may involve a panel event or brown-bag lunch series to invite diverse academics to campus.
- Make a position description as broad as possible to attract a more diverse applicant pool.
- Itemize search strategies beyond mere publication of a job announcement in order to help build a diverse applicant pool.
- Make sure all search committees have female representation and, when possible, minority representation.
- Ensure that the hiring pool contains diverse candidates before selection of finalists.
- Add an additional candidate to the finalist list if the candidate is qualified and would enhance diversity.
- Use visiting appointments or adjunct appointments to enhance faculty diversity if permanent faculty positions are unavailable.
- Recruit minority professionals interested in making a transition to the academy and support their credentialing process in what universities call "grow your own" programs.

Retention of a Diverse Faculty and Staff

Building a diverse faculty is the first step; supporting and retaining that faculty is the second step. Institutions need to support and retain *all* good faculty—White males as well as Hispanic females—and prune away any faculty who do not meet standards of quality, regardless of gender or race.

Broad-based faculty support strategies, such as faculty mentoring and flexible scheduling for those who are parents or primary caregivers, belong in a faculty development statement that applies to all. But some faculty support strategies may be directly applicable to diversity rather than to the faculty as a whole—for example, monitoring faculty salaries for gender and racial inequity or providing a private nursing area for a staff member who has a baby.

It takes both right *actions* and right *reactions* to create an environment in which diversity and inclusiveness can flourish. In recruitment, the quest for better faculty and staff diversity has a required action (seek out and hire) and a required reaction (don't discriminate). Similarly, building a culture that supports retention can involve action (encourage faculty and staff to be role models whose actions and attitudes demonstrate tolerance and respect for others) as well as reaction (respond appropriately and meaningfully to incidents and situations that are inappropriate).

One idea for measuring actions and reactions is to have a standing committee monitor a program's culture and environment as they relate to diversity. An institution could periodically gather diverse faculty and staff members and ask them about the academic culture. A university could require all newly hired faculty and staff to attend a diversity training program early in their employment to learn how to work effectively in a multicultural organization. One institution schedules a session for adjuncts to discuss creative ways in which diversity issues can be effectively communicated in the classroom.

The goal is to create an environment that embraces diversity rather than sees it as a matter of compliance. You want to not only attract diverse colleagues to your institution, but also help them be happy, comfortable, productive, and successful in navigating university life.

All faculty would benefit from colleagues occasionally visiting a class and offering constructive feedback, in the same way that faculty would benefit from observing one another and seeing what works for others. Build this sort of interaction into the system so that new and minority faculty feel less isolated.

A department chair who sees course evaluations should read those of new faculty and diverse faculty first because those faculty may be the most impacted by what students say, especially if a few students make negative comments about a teacher's mannerisms, personal characteristics, body type, or dress. In fact, empirical studies have shown that minority faculty members tend to receive lower student evaluations than their White colleagues, sometimes with direct references to gender, race, or ethnicity (Merritt, 2012). Department chairs can work closely with faculty to address student comments that appear to be based on inappropriate criteria for evaluation or unfair criticism.

Pay attention to the diversity reflected on panels and in public settings. Diverse faculty and staff will be more likely to stay at an institution that publicly recognizes and values its diversity. For instance, a university realized on the eve of a major campus event that everyone scheduled to be on the podium was a White male. By realizing this in advance, the school was able to modify the participant group to better reflect the diversity that actually existed.

In sum, consider the following list of best practices for faculty retention:

- Establish a culture that embraces diversity, which will require proper actions and reactions.
- Monitor faculty and staff salaries for gender and racial inequities.
- Have a standing committee periodically gather the perspectives of underrepresented faculty on ways to improve the campus environment.
- Create an expectation that all new faculty and staff will attend a diversity workshop within the first year or host one in your own unit.
- Schedule a session for adjunct faculty to discuss creative ways to communicate diversity issues in the classroom.
- Monitor student evaluations for harmful comments, and visit classes to offer useful feedback.
- Be cognizant of the diversity (or lack of it) reflected in panels and public events.

Conclusion

The road to inclusion is really an intersection.

The recruitment and retention of faculty and staff often fail to acknowledge the intersectionality among diverse communities. Rather than being singular dimensions, categories such as gender, race, ethnicity, sexuality, disability, age, religious belief, and social class can overlap and intersect in dynamic ways that shape each individual (Kelly, 2014).

A Bentley University report concluded that "if individuals cannot be their authentic selves in their organizations, they will not be as engaged, will not thrive, and may in fact leave" (Goux, 2012). The report added that millennials are particularly seen as valuing the multiplicity of their identities—the *whole* self—as opposed to just the conventional delineations to which they belong.

In the end, the recruitment and retention of a diverse faculty and staff are about creating a place that is good for all—faculty, staff, students, and society.

References

ASJMC Diversity Committee (2008). *Diversity revisited: Good ideas for your diversity plan.* Association of Schools of Journalism and Mass Communication. Retrieved from http://www.asjmc.org/resources/diversity_booklet/index.php

Goux, D. (2012). *Millennials in the workplace.* Retrieved from https://www.bentley .edu/centers/sites/www.bentley.edu.centers/files/centers/cwb/millennials-report.pdf

Kelly, W., & Smith, C. (2014, December 11). *What if the road to inclusion were really an intersection?* Retrieved from http://dupress.com/articles/multidimensional-diversity

Lynch, M. (2013, April 24). Diversity in college faculty just as important as student body. Retrieved from http://diverseeducation.com/article/52902

Merritt, D. (2012). Bias, the brain, and student evaluations of teaching. *St. John's Law Review, 82*(1), 235–288.

Salomon-Fernandez, Y. (2015, April 1). Beyond the NLRB ruling in favor of adjunct faculty. Retrieved from https://www.insidehighered.com/blogs/university-venus/beyond-nlrb-ruling-favor-adjunct-faculty

Smith, W., & Bender, T. (Eds.). (2008). *American higher education transformed, 1940–2005: Documenting the national discourse.* Baltimore, MD: Johns Hopkins University Press.

Urban Universities for HEALTH. (2015). *Faculty cluster hiring for diversity and institutional climate.* Retrieved from http://urbanuniversitiesforhealth.org/media/documents/Faculty_Cluster Hiring_Report.pdf

U.S. Department of Education. (2013). *Postsecondary enrollment.* Washington, DC: National Center for Education Statistics. Retrieved from http://nces.ed.gov/fastfacts/display.asp?id=98

U.S. Department of Education. (2014). *Race/ethnicity of college faculty.* Washington, DC: National Center for Education Statistics. Retrieved from https://nces.ed.gov/fastfacts/display.asp?id=61

3

LEADERSHIP AT THE INTERSECTION

A Developmental Framework for Inclusive Leaders

Niki Latino

Who you are as an individual impacts who you become as a leader. Each one of us has been socialized in a world where we consciously and subconsciously acquire biases, assumptions, and prejudices. Inclusive leaders work actively against these limitations to become more inclusive individuals and, ultimately, more inclusive leaders. They take shared ownership and shared responsibility for advancing diversity and inclusive excellence to create environments in which everyone feels welcomed, affirmed, and valued. These inclusive environments offer access and opportunity for everyone to achieve their full human potential (Tatum, 1997).

Transformative inclusive leaders must recognize the ways in which personal intersections of identity, the dilemmas facing higher education, and important social justice principles should shape how decisions are made and how society advances. If leaders faced with these issues are to perform with integrity, they must understand how their personal lenses impact their professional practices. Historically, and still today, leaders from traditionally marginalized identities (e.g., those related to race, sexual orientation, disability, gender) shoulder the responsibility for transforming college campuses to be more inclusive. Inclusive excellence challenges everyone on campus to take shared responsibility for this critical transformation (Williams, Berger, & McClendon, 2005).

Inclusive excellence, a term developed by the American Association of Colleges and Universities (AAC&U) (Williams et al., 2005), embodies a practice of shifting the responsibility for advancing diversity and excellence initiatives and actions away from a single person or office to an infusion of responsibility across campus. This chapter draws on research grounded in this framework to help educators (i.e., faculty, staff, administrators) learn how to become more effective partners in the work of transforming college campuses into more inclusive learning environments.

This study on inclusive leadership for White college administrators, with implications for educators with other privileged identities (e.g., male, heterosexual, affluent, able-bodied), focused on how 11 White college administrators who work at a predominantly White institution (PWI) became inclusive leaders and took shared ownership and responsibility for inclusive excellence (Latino, 2010). These White inclusive leaders have helped to advance the concepts of inclusive excellence, including access, improving the campus climate, and developing more inclusive policies and procedures. They were identified by students, faculty, and/or staff as people who articulated the values of inclusive leadership and applied these principles in their professional practice. The results of this study produced a framework that serves as a developmental guide for educators to examine their own personal identities, including their assumptions, biases, and prejudices, evaluate the dilemmas on their campuses, and reconstruct themselves and their educational context to reflect inclusive excellence. In addition, this study underscores the importance of how educators who become inclusive leaders develop a more critical consciousness through the intentional examination of privileged identities.

The next section briefly explores the foundational literature that contributes to inclusive leadership. An explanation of the inclusive leadership framework follows, and the chapter concludes with recommendations for practical application of this framework for inclusive leaders.

Foundational Literature

The main bodies of literature that inform the analysis of inclusive leadership for White college educators and those with other privileged identities are outlined in this section. First, the literature on critical race theory provides the foundation for making visible the social construction of race that society "invents, manipulates, and retires when convenient" (Delgado & Stefancic, 2001, p. 8). Second, literature on the construction of Whiteness, including White racial and ethnic identity as well as White privilege, explores how a White educator may learn about his or her own personal racial identity. Inclusive excellence and transformative learning research highlights the learning, unlearning, and relearning of Whiteness, as well as other privileged identities, as both a social group and a personal racial identity. Studies on privilege demonstrate the necessity of inclusive leaders developing a critical consciousness by intentionally examining their dominant identities. Third, studies of higher education leadership, including a few on inclusive leadership, supply context to this work.

Inclusive Leadership

As educators strive to become more inclusive leaders, the inclusive leadership framework may serve as a visual guide to better understand this developmental process. The framework consists of the following overarching categories: (a) four developmental phases (normalizing inclusiveness, performing inclusiveness, embracing inclusiveness, and living inclusiveness) that represent the journey of an inclusive leader, (b) four processes (discourse, self-reflexivity, meaning making, and praxis) that facilitate the growth of inclusive leaders through the developmental phases, and (c) transformative life experiences (exposure, intersections of identity, and mentors/personal relationships) that inspire a personal/emotional connection to the intellectual/political understanding of the journey. For a visual representation of the inclusive leadership framework, see Figure 3.1.

Figure 3.1 Inclusive leadership framework

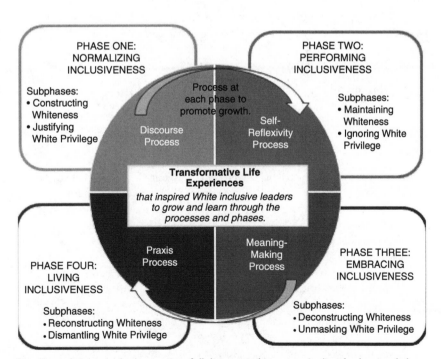

Note. Figure shows a visual representation of all three overarching categories (i.e., developmental phases, processes, and transformative life experiences) and how the categories work together.

It is important to acknowledge that one may experience stages prior to the first phase of this framework; however, the purpose of this section is to provide guidance for inclusive leaders in the *normalizing* to *living inclusiveness* phases. The first two developmental phases of *normalizing* and *performing* are intellectual, political, and professional. The second two developmental phases of *embracing* and *living* move a leader from understanding the intellectual, political, and professional importance of the inclusive leadership journey to understanding the emotional and more personal relevance of that journey. Like other developmental models, this framework is not a linear guide. Indeed, educators may experience any of the phases throughout their journey depending on the context in which they find themselves. This is a lifelong process of learning, unlearning, and relearning in the quest to become more inclusive leaders. While the focus of the framework is on White identity, there are implications for how this may manifest with other privileged identities.

Case Studies: Inclusive Leaders at the Different Phases

The following excerpts, adapted from the research, are composite voices that illustrate what an inclusive leader may experience in each phase of the framework. Reading through the composite voices encourages reflection on one's own personal journey to becoming an inclusive leader.

Normalizing Inclusiveness: Race and Ethnicity

Reflections of an inclusive leader at the *normalizing* phase:

> I know that inclusive excellence is an important concept with the changing demographics in society. I attend trainings and I listen to the information that is presented; however, I also remind myself that issues of racial discrimination at this campus were not my fault. I try not to become defensive. After all, I did not receive any special treatment because I was a White administrator at a PWI. I was treated the same as everyone else. My hard work and credibility are why I am recognized. I never had a problem with race since it was never discussed in my family except for a few negative comments toward people of color, in particular the Black community. Those comments were just part of that generation. Times have changed. Everyone gets that inclusiveness is important now. We are all expected to assimilate into this institution's culture. We have come a long way with the work that we have done as an institution.

An inclusive leader at the *normalizing* phase can understand on an intellectual level the importance of diversity and inclusiveness. Yet, the privilege that is inherited simply because of how the leader identifies remains invisible. Because their personal and environmental privilege remains invisible, leaders risk continuing to perpetuate discrimination through exclusive practice.

Performing Inclusiveness: Lesbian, Gay, Bisexual, Transgender, Intersex, Queer (LGBTIQ)

Reflections of an inclusive leader at the *performing* phase:

> I am always thinking about how to embed inclusive excellence in this department. Since it has become important to this community college, I know that I will be evaluated on what I am doing. I am working with my staff to make sure that they have all been trained on the concept by the chief diversity officer. Inclusive excellence is also mandated in performance evaluations. Unfortunately, without this mandate many of my heterosexual staff members do not engage. I do not want any negative attitudes to reflect poorly on the work being done in my area even though I do understand their attitudes; it seems overwhelming to try to be inclusive and excellent at the same time. Sometimes I become exhausted, and I need to take a break from inclusive excellence to reenergize and refocus. Yet, I do understand the importance of having a more diverse staff and more diverse ideas even if we are giving up some of the intimacy that we have when everyone is from the same identities. Maybe if we work hard, we will be recognized for our work, and other areas that are not working as hard as we are will have consequences.

An inclusive leader at the *performing* phase can understand on an intellectual, political, and professional level the importance of diversity and inclusiveness in the work environment. In this phase, there is intentional thought, planning, and implementation for advancing inclusive excellence; however, it is primarily due to the perceived rewards to that specific individual and the specific department. The privileged identity still remains invisible, which in turn impacts the changes that are made in that area.

Embracing Inclusiveness: Gender Identity

Reflections of an inclusive leader at the *embracing* phase:

> My mind and my heart are now entwined because I finally realized the privilege that I have inherited just because I am a male in the United States. Part of my privilege is to not have to think about the privilege that I have as a male or the role that I play in benefitting from systems that were intentionally created to be exclusive. We all have different experiences and journeys. I am inspired to be more intentional about reexamining my privileged iden-

tity and how this privileged identity impacts my professional practice at this large public institution. Part of my journey to connect my mind and my heart initially occurred from trying to understand why I experienced discrimination because of one aspect of my identity that is constructed as "marginalized" in this society. This painful experience and assistance from my mentor have served as fertile ground for me to better identify and understand discrimination, including sexism. Inclusive excellence, for me, has moved from something that I have to do to being about the right thing to do. No one should experience being constructed as an outsider on this campus or in our society because of one part of their identity.

Inclusive leaders at the *embracing* phase have made an emotional connection to the importance of unmasking their privileged identities. Inclusiveness is relevant intellectually and emotionally. Unfortunately, there will always be something about each of us that falls out of constructed "norms" in society. Noting transformative life experiences and how socialization in this society contributes to our biases, assumptions, and prejudices are critical transformations in connecting our minds and our hearts with the importance of inclusive leadership.

Living Inclusiveness: Religion

Reflections of an inclusive leader at the *living* phase:

Being inclusive is an inherent part of who I am. My heart is fully engaged in working to dismantle systems of privilege at this predominantly Christian institution. I understand that I have shared responsibility and shared ownership in transforming this environment to be more inclusive. Institutions were founded to be exclusive so we all have shared responsibility for transforming this environment to be more inclusive. Balancing personal accountability with professional accountability is essential in transforming my area as well as serving as an authentic partner on multicultural alliances to transform the entire campus. I use my privilege as an insider to make change. I do take intentional risks and make intentional compromises in an effort to work daily to challenge the status quo that has been established at this university. I know that we are going to have to navigate through politics and resistance because of the misperception and fear that we will lose privilege that we unfairly inherited because of our dominant identities.

I work every day making visible my personal biases and prejudices because I am very much aware that my personal beliefs and values significantly influence my professional practice. Inclusiveness is an interconnected part of being a leader and an educator for me; without one I cannot successfully have the others. Everyone deserves to be a welcomed and valued member of this community.

An inclusive leader at the *living* phase understands that everyone has a personal and a social identity. The focus becomes about authentically engaging as partners on multicultural alliances. Inclusiveness is interconnected with who the person is as a leader and as an educator. It is an intentional choice on a daily basis to unlearn historical messages and to reconstruct a more accurate truth and reality. When inclusiveness becomes a habitual part of our behavior, we can make sustainable change in which inclusive excellence is the fabric of learning environments.

The process of developing into more inclusive leaders is both rewarding and challenging. We may find ourselves continuously experiencing the various stages of the inclusive leadership framework throughout our journey because of the unlearning and relearning that we have the responsibility to engage in. It is an intentional choice on a daily basis to engage in this process as we work together to create inclusive campus environments where every individual feels welcomed, valued, and affirmed. Inclusive environments inspire the most creative thinking, problem solving, communication, and analysis. These are only a few examples of the essential skills that we teach our students as we develop competent change agents, leaders, and citizens for this global society. Some leaders might be more naturally inclined toward this type of introspective work. Some leaders will have already honed their stories through life experience or a naturally pluralistic orientation. For others, these will be new ways of thinking and new habits of mind. However, it is clear that more and more institutions will expect future educators to also lead in this area.

Recommendations for Inclusive Leadership in Practice

Best Practices and Action Steps ✓

Personal

1. Question—intentionally and often—how and why we label or assign labels to people based on our assumptions, biases, and prejudices. Listen to how people identify themselves rather than assigning identities.
2. Understand your own personal story. We tell stories in daily conversations, and our stories shape our truth and our reality.
3. Learn how your intersections of identity (e.g., gender, sexual orientation, social class) have influenced your worldview and sense of reality.
4. Do not be afraid to make mistakes as part of this process. Learning about our mistakes and experiences inspires continued personal growth and development. Keep in mind that we are all works-in-progress trying to grow and develop through a challenging journey together.

5. Create space for challenging discourse. Too often, political correctness is used as an excuse to not engage in difficult dialogue. Engaging in respectful, honest dialogue is critical in practicing inclusive leadership.

6. Examine the intent of your actions to determine if there could be a negative impact that might apply to any decision. As leaders, our decisions may be made with the best intentions, but failing to intentionally examine our privilege may have unintended consequences.

7. Do not use guilt as an excuse to avoid exploring the construction of privileged identities and one's own personal privilege. Each of us as an individual is not responsible for changing past history; however, we have a shared responsibility to transform present and future contexts.

8. Reexamine the messages learned in your historical contexts and experiences that shaped your initial understanding of privilege and your personal identities. This type of self-reflection can be explored through conversations with colleagues, reading social media posts, journaling, commenting on one's own and others' biases and assumptions about race/ethnicity, and narrating your story in various professional arenas.

9. Identify and understand your participation in systems of racial privilege in a predominantly White environment.

10. Do not take breaks from working toward inclusive excellence. People from nonmajority groups cannot take breaks from being in a group that is oppressed. Taking breaks can be disguised in a variety of attractive excuses, including self-care. Once the meaning making is connected to the heart, breaks are no longer an option. When leaders with privileged identities take breaks, leaders who are not part of the dominant group must continue to shoulder the responsibility. Inclusiveness is everyone's responsibility, and breaks for privileged identities cannot be an option. That being said, true self-care is important for anyone doing diversity and inclusion work, no matter their identity.

11. Allow your transformative life experiences to be doors and windows into greater and deeper understanding by intentionally engaging in critical discourse and self-reflexivity about these experiences.

Professional

1. Walk the talk. If inclusive excellence is a core value, then develop tangible action plans to embed this value in mission statements and strategic plans. Include financial resources and assessment to make the appropriate changes. Making materials public is another form of accountability.

2. Engage with campus partners, such as disability services, international student services, multicultural affairs, LGBTIQ services, religious organizations,

and gender and women's studies departments, to review written materials, websites, policies, and programs to determine whether the language is accessible for and inclusive of all identities.

3. Create an environment that encourages constructive feedback regarding inclusive practices.
4. Do not leave your inclusiveness at work (i.e., do not perform inclusiveness only during the workday). Purposefully commit to identifying ways to be more personally inclusive.
5. Empower your staff members to achieve inclusive excellence through professional development as well as educational opportunities.
6. Create individual inclusive excellence plans for each member in the department/division to continuously reflect upon their personal and professional actions. Create an inclusive excellence "toolkit" with questions for departments to annually review their progress, including evaluations of monetary resources, professional development, mission, strategic planning, physical environment, and assessment.
7. Use a variety of levels of action to build momentum for change. For example, include inclusive excellence in job descriptions and performance evaluations, encourage and support staff in attending professional and educational development opportunities, and be purposeful in establishing achievable goals.
8. Negotiate challenging the system while working within the system. Remember, it is about rocking the boat, not ejecting yourself from the boat. You need to be in the boat to make changes as an insider.
9. Identify colleagues who are working toward building sustainable momentum for change and develop partnerships within and across departments and divisions and throughout the campus community.
10. Recognize that transforming an environment into an inclusive one is a gradual journey. When intentional steps are taken daily, change occurs over time.

Conclusion

In our quest to become more inclusive leaders, it is critical to remember that our personal identities influence our professional practices. This is a lifelong journey that is challenging, rewarding, and necessary for us to create inclusive environments that are representative of our ever-evolving diverse and global society. Silence and inaction by educators with privileged identities should no longer be options. Instead, we need to work together as authentic partners on multicultural alliances to create sustainable change, because our students deserve an inclusively excellent learning environment.

As inclusive leaders, we should strive to create learning environments that cultivate competent, committed citizens and leaders for a global society. However, we cannot and should not expect anything of our students that we are not modeling ourselves. At the core of this process is connecting the mind and the heart to move from viewing inclusive excellence and diversity as concepts with which one is expected to engage to viewing them as inherently right; an environment that is exclusive to anyone is negative for everyone (Feagin, Vera, & Batur, 2000). A campus community with inclusion as the fabric of the learning environment, both inside and outside the classroom, facilitates excellence. In fact, in its inclusive excellence change model, the AAC&U further explained that diversity is

> a key component of a comprehensive strategy for achieving institutional excellence—which includes, but is not limited to, the academic excellence of all students in attendance and concerted efforts to educate all students to succeed in a diverse society and equip them with sophisticated intercultural skills. (Williams, Berger, & McClendon, 2005, p. 3)

Making visible the benefit of an inclusive campus is essential to combating the misperception that something will be lost if change occurs.

Educators with privileged identities have to take shared ownership and shared responsibility to partner in dismantling the status quo. It is not right or just for only people from traditionally marginalized identities to continue to shoulder this responsibility. Johnson (2001) maintained that "to have privilege is to be allowed to move through your life without being marked in ways that identify you as an outsider, as exceptional or 'other' to be excluded, or to be included but always with conditions" (p. 33).

If we do not make the choice to intentionally engage, we continue to perpetuate systems of exclusion and oppression. Through silence and inaction, we remain part of the problem. By working together as authentic partners to create sustainable change, we are creating more productive educational experiences to provide the knowledge, education, skills, and training to develop current and future agents of change. Together we can transform exclusive environments into inclusive campus communities where everyone feels welcomed, affirmed, and valued.

References

Baumann, G., Bustillos, L. T., Bensimon, E. N., & Bartee, R. (2005). *Achieving equitable outcomes with all students: The institution's roles and responsibilities.* Washington, DC: American Association of Colleges and Universities.

Delgado, R., & Stefancic, J. (2001). *Critical race theory: The cutting edge.* Philadelphia, PA: Temple University Press.

Feagin, J., Vera, H., & Batur, P. (2000). *White racism* (2nd ed.). New York, NY: Routledge.

Johnson, A. (2001). *Privilege, power, and difference* (2nd ed.). New York, NY: McGraw-Hill

Latino, N. M. (2010). *Unmasking Whiteness: A framework for understanding inclusive leadership at a predominantly White institution* (Doctoral dissertation). Retrieved from ProQuest Dissertations and Theses. (ED521276)

Milem, J., Chang, M., & Antonio, A. (2005). *Making excellence inclusive: A research-based perspective.* Washington, DC: American Association of Colleges and Universities.

Tatum, B. (1997). Racial identity development and relational theory: The case of Black women in White communities. In J. Jordan (Ed.), *Women's growth in diversity* (pp. 91–107). New York, NY: Guilford Press.

Williams, D., Berger, J., & McClendon, S. (2005). *Toward a model of inclusive excellence and change in postsecondary institutions.* Washington, DC: American Association of Colleges and Universities.

4

LEADERS, GOVERNING BODIES, AND ADVISORY BOARDS

Jeff Stein and Leo M. Lambert

L ike living organisms, colleges and universities must evolve to remain competitive and relevant in the rapidly changing economy. Little in the ecosystems within and without our institutions remains stable. Leaders, governing bodies, and advisory boards are developing and implementing strategic plans as national and international debates rage on topics from immigration reform to gay marriage in an environment of ISIS videos of beheadings in the Middle East and Black males shot and killed by police in cities across the country. These issues are only magnified on college campuses, where people from a diverse range of ethnicities, nationalities, religions, political views, disciplines, and perspectives interact in a tightly knit, 24/7 environment.

Often the problems in the wider world boil over into campus conflicts that force boards and leaders into the position of arbiters. To succeed in this climate, president of Arizona State University Michael Crow (2010) argued, decision makers must "offer access to excellence to a broad demographic range of students" while simultaneously "[seek] solutions to global challenges." At many institutions, students, faculty, staff, parents, and board members embrace the vision of preparing students to become global citizens able to navigate complexities of languages, cultures, and worldviews. However, colleges and universities are intricate webs of intersecting institutional histories, values, demographic groups, purposes, and market forces. In order to create substantive and effective strategic plans for achieving these ambitious inclusivity goals, governing boards and campus leaders must maintain a laser-like focus on strategic planning based on a shared vision, common concepts of leadership and accountability, expertise and deep involvement of

will progress, how everyone will be impacted, or how lives or work will be altered. This can be disturbing for some, and it requires listening, transparency, ongoing communication, and clear language. Before the gates open, create clear messages and design processes for gathering feedback from all constituents. After the plan launches, providing regular updates is essential.

A majority of your constituents already agree on the power of higher education, particularly the education from your instution. Most people want to make this transformative experience available to as many young people as possible, preparing them for success in a globally competitive age. Consequently, begin your work by allowing those invested in your college or university to describe why this education should be available to more students. Every strategic planning process should include a multitude of opportunities for students, alumni, parents, staff, faculty, and board members to weigh in on the institution's trajectory as well as on how the mission statement continues to guide and drive the university forward in the most comprehensive sense. Constituents should provide feedback on existing institutional structures and programs and describe what is missing. They will not agree wholeheartedly on every issue. This range of opinions will force you to make choices and create a complex and nuanced plan.

Use every communication platform at your disposal to inform and update constituents about strategic plan development and progress. Focus groups, listening groups, e-mail accounts specifically for accepting feedback, letters or videos inviting feedback, surveys, and whiteboards posted around campus with questions related to potential goals are helpful. Public relations staff can easily create and coordinate e-mail and online surveys to on- and off-campus constituents. Internal and external audiences can rank and comment on potential future initiatives and stretch goals as well. Online articles; feature stories in the college or university magazine; update letters or e-mails from the president, provost, and chief diversity officer; and meetings among senior administrators and departments, divisions, student groups, faculty, and staff keep constituents up-to-date and create a steady drumbeat of information. Discontent can fester when audiences do not have access to facts; keep institutional communication transparent and specifically focused on your work to increase buy-in from a wide range of constituencies.

Clearly articulate your plan with precise language that addresses concerns shared by all constituents and does not rely on buzzwords. Finding the right specific and bold language, though, is not merely about avoiding confusion. *Diversity* remains a misunderstood and loaded term with a great deal of unintended baggage. If the goal is to help students prepare for twenty-first-century jobs, which may very well be outside of the United States, make that clear early. If the concern is how students will manage differences in language, culture, nationality, religious traditions, and political and economic structures, then say so. Be specific and direct. Articulate strategic goals simply. State that you plan to "double need-based financial aid," "provide 100% study abroad access," or "triple international student enrollment," for example (Elon University, 2014). Particularly with issues as complex as diversity and inclusion, help your constituents to support your goals and explain them to others.

In the same vein, never assume stakeholders understand these goals or know why these initiatives are important. Explain to audiences how plans dovetail with academic purposes and impact real people. Plans should be written in the realm of academic outcomes that explain the value of diversity of thought. The preamble to *A Diversity Action Plan for Brown University* (Office of the Associate Provost and Director of Institutional Diversity, 2006) opens by addressing why the plan matters: "Students educated in diverse environments have been found to learn better, to deal with complexity more readily, and to emerge with a greater understanding of how to participate productively in a pluralistic society" (p. 3). Plans should also be substantiated with the vast body of research proving the positive impact of diversity on complex thinking, students' need for diverse learning environments in order to tackle the highest-order tasks, and persistence of these outcomes after graduation as alumni engage in their communities. In addition to the research, strategic plans should allow readers to imagine the potential outcomes through student and alumni profiles and stories that illustrate the impact on real people.

Of course, it is one thing to know that all constituents believe in the importance of global study and keeping college affordable. It is a completely different matter to understand where community members disagree and the difference between stretch goals and extremes that may alienate certain constituents. No matter the audience, strategic diversity initiatives will encounter skeptics. Even constituents who fully support your goals may struggle with terminology or assume the worst—that you have gone to political extremes far from the shared goals you have worked so hard to identify, that your efforts are cursory or "drive-by" diversity, or, even worse, that your intentions are not to act but merely to pay lip service to placate certain groups.

Hence, the listening and engagement do not end once the plan is unveiled. Just continue communicating. After introducing strategic plans, constituents will express different concerns and continue to provide advice. Instead of becoming defensive, listen when students, faculty, staff, alumni, parents, or trustees—even those who wholeheartedly want diversity in the strategic plan—express concerns. This advice will help you understand the boundaries of your work, the need to communicate your goals more clearly, and the fear that any change process unearths.

Transparency about goals and progress is essential. If necessary, external consultants can challenge and support leadership teams in this process and provide examples and ideas from a range of institutions and industries. Annual presentations to boards, governing bodies, alumni, parents, and friends of the institution; annual addresses to faculty and staff; meetings with student groups; progress reports on your website; board and council discussions of short white papers outlining specific programs or challenges; and midpoint retreats all maintain the work's visibility. The goal is for everyone at your institution to be able to articulate the plan. Clarifying and staying on message and seeing their interests in your efforts—as opposed to shifting off course in meetings or creating obstacles, such as social media sniping—keep boards, councils, and alumni supporting your work. Conflicting, confusing, or ambiguous messages can derail any strategic process. Consistent and precise messaging and goals grounded in clear and familiar contexts ensure that your community understands your targets and is less apt to imagine crises or conflicts that you never intended.

Governing Bodies and Advisory Boards

It is essential to keep governing boards and councils at the forefront of the change process. Nationally, governing board demographics have not changed significantly over time. Although a majority of college students are women, and the country's population is shifting toward a majority of people of color, governing boards across the country remain predominantly White and male. About 70% of all board members are male, 74% of public board members are White, and 87% of private board members are White, according to the Association of Governing Boards' study of board composition, policies, and practices (Schwartz, 2010). Based on these demographics, some campus leaders doubt the will of governing bodies to support campus access and inclusion efforts.

Nivet and Berlin (2014), on the other hand, explained in "Diversity Questions for Boards" that inclusive climate issues are at the core of what governing boards already consider. Boards are naturally concerned with the effectiveness of your institution, including yield and graduation rates for students, as well as with faculty promotion and tenure. Board members are advocates for consistent "productivity across all subpopulation and identity groups" (Nivet & Berlin, 2014). They value the school's reputation for fairness and the preparation and accomplishments of alumni. Because governing boards consider future strategies part of their natural function, their members are usually well acquainted with discussing many of these questions, key institutional needs and assets, and the big ideas for the next strategic plan.

Boards can also become more skilled at this work, just as they learn to navigate other idiosyncrasies of higher education. Two of the many questions Nivet and Berlin posed to help boards understand their roles in supporting diversity are: "Is the institution's educational approach working equally for students across all subpopulations and identity groups?" and "Is the institution graduating students with the skill sets needed to succeed in a pluralistic society?" (Nivet & Berlin, 2014). According to Richard Meyers (2010), president of Fielding Graduate University, numerous strategies exist for boards to engage these issues, including simply setting aside time to consider diversity questions, issues, and perspectives. President Jonathan Alger of James Madison University identified three clear imperatives that compel boards to focus on diversity. Alger's social and moral imperative drives boards to "provide access to higher education for people who historically have not had it" (Association of Governing Boards of Universities and Colleges, 2014). The economic imperative motivates boards to consider developing "diverse human capital . . . to its full potential" in order to keep the country competitive in world markets. Finally, Alger (Association of Governing Boards of Universities and Colleges, 2014) suggested that the educational imperative proves that diversity benefits all learning environments and students. Thus, campuses should not hesitate to deeply engage boards and councils in the process of thinking about fairness, productivity, and completion.

In order to keep boards engaged in and updated on inclusion efforts, include members on strategic planning committees; include students, staff, and faculty panels in board meetings; provide and lead discussion on short, thought-provoking white papers; discuss relevant issues during committee meetings; connect students and board members over social activities such as meals; and regularly review specific data from dashboards and reports regarding these goals. Data should be specific and placed in the context of the board's fiduciary responsibility and the choices they have been asked to make in the past.

Most importantly, tap into board members' expertise. They are sophisticated leaders in their fields, chosen specifically for their abilities to lead, their support of the institution, and their dedication to ensuring the health of your institution. Many leading organizations with which your board members are affiliated developed forward-thinking practices for customer service and employee relations long ago, in order to meet the needs of the market. For example, some Elon trustees provided advice on how they handled concerns about partner benefits as the institution approached the issue. Board members can be your best advocates and consultants.

A trustee once articulated this function to our senior leaders, saying, "My job is to make you think scary thoughts." According to this trustee, boards and councils push administrators to consider future risks, to imagine greater challenges, and to keep plans and goals both sharp and audacious. Ideally, these groups have the distance from the day-to-day operations to keep senior leaders focused on bold stretch goals that take your breath away a bit while remaining within the realm of feasibility. Let board members keep you sharp and help you reach your goals. Elon's experience with generous board support for our multifaith center (when other constituents were supporting religious and spiritual life programs aligned with their own personal affiliations) provides an example of an instance when impartial board members with broader institutional loyalties were the primary supporters of an inclusivity initiative.

Institutional Leadership, Structures, and Accountability

Governing bodies also keep campus leaders focused on structural concerns, such as budgets, leadership, and crisis response models. When we presented early drafts of the Elon Commitment Strategic Plan to boards and councils without a clear leader identified for the diversity and global engagement initiatives, one member quickly responded that if no one person was in charge, then the plans would not succeed. And, of course, this member was right.

Leadership matters. It takes time to develop a leadership structure and model, especially when many campus leaders are already committed to existing aspects of diversity education and supporting specific populations. The focus should be on hiring the best-quality people who will raise the level of the department and institution. In support of Elon's strategic plan, during the last five years, we have added key leaders to take ownership for aspects of the plan, including a chief diversity officer; a director of the Gender & LGBTQIA Center; additional staff supporting access and success programs; additional staff in the Center for Race, Ethnicity, and Diversity Education; staff supporting African American and Hispanic/Latin@ students; additional employee-relations staff in human resources; and more.

Create an organizational structure to effectively connect the leaders and offices that are currently working independently with specific identity groups. Your goal is to align the staff focused on individual groups into a greater whole in order to make progress on larger institutional inclusion goals and also to assist students who may find themselves at the intersections of identity groups. Decide early and communicate clearly which staff members are in charge and accountable for the success of each initiative, particularly because staff and faculty are already working with some aspect of diversity and feel responsible for its success. Define reporting lines and accountability and create a mechanism, under either the chief academic officer or chief student affairs officer, for leaders to come together to work collaboratively and communicate regularly.

Intersections of identity and larger institutional goals also require attention from coordinating teams that meet regularly and include a wide range of leaders working with areas such as race and ethnicity, access and success, gender and sexual orientation, religion and worldview, disability services, and nationality and place of origin. As opposed to prior structures that focused inclusion work only on individual demographic groups under the auspices of individual departments, contemporary diversity and inclusion efforts are more successful when infused throughout campus from top-level leadership (including senior leaders and a chief diversity officer) and coordinated with broader campus staff and organizations. This coordination of campus offices allows inclusion staff to consider support for students with multiple identities, to analyze where efforts or issues overlap on campus, and to collaborate on larger institutional goals.

Accountability measures can help to ensure this work is stitched across campus. For example, the Swarthmore College Diversity and Inclusion Implementation Committee's 2013 report suggested that "each department and office will be required to include in its end-of-the-year report a discussion of how it contributed to the goal of creating a diverse and inclusive learning environment." Initiatives should be woven throughout all schools, colleges, and divisions at the institution, including academics, admissions, human resources, university communications, student affairs, campus safety and police, construction and design, technology, and athletics. Budgets and resources must also be tied to these initiatives. Unless your institution already has or receives the funds to fully support the work, it is often more realistic to invest significantly in these priorities systematically over time, always ensuring that support remains a focus for fund-raising. Some institutions also require employees to address diversity and inclusion in their annual performance reviews, as well as in their goals for professional development. Another accountability technique is to publish annual institutional priorities and list the names of the responsible campus leaders next to each priority. Midyear and end-of-year reports addressing progress on priorities are good reminders for responsible campus leaders, as well as the entire campus.

Moving Forward and Managing Ongoing Challenges

No matter how well we develop inclusivity plans, institutional leaders and boards will be challenged to effectively respond to issues and events that threaten campus inclusivity and global engagement. In this volatile social media era, issues can take hold of your campus at lightning speed and permeate the airspace for lengthy periods. Clear emergency plans, advance trainings, response plans and teams, constant listening to constituents, and careful attention to town-gown relations and external groups are needed to weather these contemporary storms.

A full range of professional development resources and sessions for all levels of expertise is needed to ensure that campus faculty and staff can update and deepen their knowledge and skills on everything from infusing diversity into the curriculum to supporting the needs of diverse students and colleagues. A more challenging task is to be prepared for skepticism, conflict, increased reporting of incidents of bias, and attempts by both internal and external audiences to shift focus away from inclusion initiatives with nostalgia for old ways of doing business. This work is inherently challenging and requires constant dialogue on campus. Conflicts and tensions are inevitable as individuals and groups jockey for position, think more deeply about issues of inclusion and belonging, and gain skill in thinking and talking about difference. Highly skilled faculty and staff are needed to process these differences in a sophisticated manner, listen to concerns, support those in need, and ensure that issues do not boil over.

Senseless acts of hate and disrespect will occur on campus. In these instances, senior leaders, faculty, and staff must rely on clearly defined campus protocols and respond swiftly with a unified voice that such actions are antithetical to institutional values. Do not be surprised when off-campus groups, representing a wide range of views, attempt to use campus incidents and social media to drum up controversies and create their own bully pulpits. National and international issues and incidents—presidential elections, protests, state ballot initiatives, Supreme Court cases, wars, shootings, violent altercations—will also tear at the fabric of your campus community.

When the leader of a national fast-food chain used social media to promote particular beliefs about marriage, politicized rhetoric disrupted schools across the country. Campuses experienced constituent calls, student government debates, student votes on removing the chain as a campus vendor, heated campus dialogues, and national media exposure. It became clear that many campuses lacked the structures to facilitate effective civic dialogue and teach students how to address controversial issues. On our campus, a committee of students, faculty, staff, alumni, and trustees spent months listening, researching, interviewing, and developing recommendations for moving forward and for implementing dialogue programs that teach students how to engage when they disagree. Social media forces institutions to be ready to respond instantaneously to a wide range of potential threats to individuals, groups, and the community as a whole, as well as to respond with methods for bringing constituents together to talk about conflicts. Well-trained personnel who can remain on-message, communicate clearly, and follow clear response protocols will help when eventual crises hit.

Conclusion

Supporting intersectional identities is inherently complex and requires careful planning and communication. This work draws together intersections of institutional history and values, core campus programs, competencies for the global economy, and both academic and student affairs personnel. Inclusion work cannot be conducted with disconnected campus offices focusing on individual demographic groups. Instead, colleges and universities must, as Mildred García, the president of California State University, argues "redouble . . . efforts to ensure that all students learn with and from diverse peers and graduate ready to lead in a diverse and globally connected world" (Humphreys, 2013). Campus leaders cannot be afraid to engage governing bodies deeply in these efforts. Together, leaders and boards can develop clear plans and leadership and accountability structures to navigate the storms of social media, national debates, and political protests that eventually complicate this work. Sophisticated strategic plans based on shared vision, the expertise and deep involvement of boards and councils, defined leadership and accountability, and clear and continuous communication across institutional constituencies are all required in order to prepare students for meaningful lives in a twenty-first-century global society.

References

Association of Governing Boards of Universities and Colleges. (2014, May–June). *Why boards must become diversity stewards*. Retrieved from http://agb.org/trusteeship/2014/5/why-boards-must-become-diversity-stewards

Crow, M. M. (2010, May–June). *Toward institutional innovation in America's colleges and universities*. Retrieved from http://agb.org/trusteeship/2010/mayjune/toward-institutional-innovation-in-americas-colleges-and-universities

Elon University. (2014). *Strategic plan 2020: Diversity*. Retrieved from http://www.elon.edu/e-web/administration/president/strategicplan2020/diversity.xhtml

Guttman, A. (n.d.). *Diversity at Penn*. Retrieved from http://diversity.upenn.edu/diversity_at_penn

Humphreys, D. (2013, August 15). *Without inclusion, there is no true excellence.* Retrieved from http://www.aacu.org/press/press-releases/without-inclusion-there-no-true-excellence-aacu-board-directors-affirms-new

Meyers, R. S. (2010, July–August). *Diversity and the board.* Retrieved from http://agb.org/trusteeship/2010/julyaugust/diversity-and-the-board

Nivet, M. A., & Berlin, A. C. (2014, May–June). *Diversity questions for boards.* Retrieved from http://agb.org/trusteeship/2014/5/why-boards-must-become-diversity-stewards

Office of the Associate Provost and Director of Institutional Diversity. (2006). *A diversity action plan for Brown University.* Retrieved from https://www.brown.edu/about/administration/human-resources/sites/brown.edu.about.administration.human-resources/files/diversity-brochure.pdf

Schwartz, M. P. (2010, November–December). *How diverse are governing boards? How diverse should they be?* Retrieved from http://agb.org/trusteeship/2010/novemberdecember/how-diverse-are-governing-boards-how-diverse-should-they-be

Swarthmore College Diversity and Inclusion Implementation Committee. (2013, September 5). *Diversity and inclusion implementation committee report.* Retrieved from http://www.swarthmore.edu/Documents/stratdirections/Final.DraftDIreport.pdf

5

IT TAKES A CAMPUS

Building Capacity to Sustain the Diversity Journey

Michael A. McDonald, Sarah B. Westfall, and Eileen B. Wilson-Oyelaran

T his chapter describes the diversity and inclusion (D&I) journey that has been ongoing at Kalamazoo College during the last decade. It identifies key themes that have informed our work as a way of illustrating the successes as well as the challenges we have faced in our efforts to create a more inclusive student-focused campus community. Though each institutional context is different, we offer our experience as a case study that is applicable across a broad array of colleges and universities.

Since its inception, Kalamazoo's D&I approach has incorporated various types and levels of intersection (e.g., departmental and constituent intersections), and it is inclusive of all aspects of personal identity. The senior leadership (president's staff) leads the D&I institutional efforts and, recognizing that it impacts every aspect of our mission, brings a cross-functional, team-based approach to the work. Kalamazoo's D&I work involves colleagues with broadly diverse experience and skill sets who come from every part of campus. Moreover, as we commenced our work, we chose not to privilege any elements of personal identity over others. Colloquially we refer to "every part of every person" as a way to acknowledge the intersectional personal identities we seek to fully include. In other words, the term *intersectional* describes the multiple, differently situated campus colleagues who contribute to the work toward the full inclusion of every part of everyone on campus.

Background

Kalamazoo is a traditional residential liberal arts college of just under 1,500 students located halfway between Detroit and Chicago. In 2005, as a new president arrived, the college had less than 10% students of color, nearly no degree-seeking international students, and less than 9% Pell-eligible students. The new president was perplexed by the absence of economic, geographic, and racial diversity at Kalamazoo. During the search process, she had emphasized her personal commitment to diversity and her philosophical position that a diverse campus community is an essential component of twenty-first-century educational excellence. Shortly after her arrival, she learned that, based on the 2000 United States Census, "Michigan [was] the most segregated state in the nation. Five of the 25 most racially segregated metropolitan regions in the United States—Detroit, Saginaw, Flint, Benton Harbor, and Muskegon—[were] in Michigan. . . . Almost all of the state's Black residents . . . [lived] in just 11 metropolitan regions . . . [and] roughly 70 of the state's 83 counties [were] overwhelmingly White" (Schneider, 2003). The state's public school systems were also the most segregated in the nation, with "82 percent of Black students . . . enrolled in just three [school] districts [and] some 90 percent of White students . . . enrolled in Detroit-region schools where 10 percent or less of the students [were] Black" (Schneider, 2003). She wondered what this might mean for recruitment, given that at the time more than 70% of the student body was from Michigan, and for how students interacted once they arrived on campus.

Conversations with campus constituents revealed that the issue of diversity had been a long-standing topic of concern, study, and sometimes conflict on the campus. Why, she wondered, had so little progress occurred?

To better understand the situation, an independent assessment, called an "Inclusivity Audit," was conducted by two experienced consultants. The charge to these individuals was to assess the readiness of the college to undertake, sustain, and make significant strides in the process of becoming a more diverse and inclusive campus, and to make recommendations for specific action steps that might lead to the development of a diversity mind-set at Kalamazoo. The findings would be used to guide future action and to inform the upcoming strategic planning process.

The consultants held strategic, confidential conversations with more than 50 students, faculty, and staff, and with all members of the then executive team.[1] They also reviewed numerous reports on various aspects of diversity at Kalamazoo dating back to 1995.

For purposes of the audit and the strategic planning work that followed, we defined *diversity* as the process of developing an environment that maximizes the potential of all constituents of the college. Diversity is not a final state; rather, it is an ongoing process. In embracing this definition we recognized that diversity is not limited to ethnicity, race, and gender. Rather, it is inclusive of all group identities. Additionally, developing an environment that maximizes the potential of all people requires valuing group differences at the interpersonal and institutional levels.

The audit findings revealed that Kalamazoo had spent considerable energy and time "talking" about the importance of diversity but that very little had changed. According to the consultants, this view was informed by two main factors. First, there were very few people of color working at or attending Kalamazoo. Second, respondents did not perceive the campus climate as consistently respectful of everyone regardless of gender, race, national origin, or age. The consultants did, however, commend the college for its high-quality, in-depth analyses pertaining to diversity-related issues. They concluded in their confidential report to the president, "What is critical now is relevant action to match the rhetoric" (personal communication, 2006). Many institutions have been or will find themselves at a similar point, with unclear ideas about how to proceed but a clear idea that they must.

To assist with the transition from rhetoric to action, the consultants offered 17 recommendations focusing on the following main strategic imperatives:

- Articulate a new vision for a diverse and inclusive Kalamazoo community and effectively communicate the importance of this vision and its centrality to Kalamazoo's mission.
- Build the capacity of the leadership team and the faculty to undertake sustained diversity work and establish expectations and accountability measures related to these efforts.
- Become a more inclusive and student-focused campus.
- Ensure the college's operations (admission and financial aid strategies, curriculum design and review, hiring and onboarding practices, vendor identification and selection, etc.) reflect the college's commitment to diversity and inclusion.

In closing, the report offered some cautionary remarks:

> The new president has become the symbol of newfound confidence that cultural change can indeed be effected at last. Her presidency offers renewed hope. Can one person, of any color or gender, single-handedly revitalize and rejuvenate an institution of higher learning bound by tradition? No. Can one person change an entire campus, and all its constituencies, and especially around issues of diversity? No. (personal communication, 2006)

Consequently, the consultants recommended that the college immediately identify interim diversity leadership to undertake this work as soon as possible. A recently retired faculty member agreed to assume this role. Our initial efforts focused on enhancing the capacity of the leadership team through a series of retreats and organizing conversations among triads of diverse individuals throughout the campus who explored their experiences with diversity and their hopes for diversity and inclusion at Kalamazoo.

These efforts provided the foundation from which the strategic priority to "create a diverse and inclusive student focused campus" emerged. Central to this priority was increasing all forms of representational diversity (economic, gender, geographic, national, and racial/ethnic) among the student body and ensuring that Kalamazoo students would have an opportunity to engage with faculty and staff who reflect the international and multicultural dimensions of the twenty-first-century global community. Recognizing that systemic institutional change would be required to realize the goal of creating a diverse and inclusive campus, the plan also set the expectation that "Kalamazoo College will be an intercultural institution in which the campus community is engaged in learning across differences in a context where no culture dominates."

Philosophy

As we began our diversity journey, the college adopted an infuse-and-embed philosophy that guided both policy and practice. It is characterized by recognizing two crucial principles.

First, genuine cultural change can be achieved only if diversity work is infused and embedded into the everyday work of the institution. Diversity and inclusion work cannot be perceived as an add-on for an already very busy campus community. Institutional leaders must develop a diversity mind-set that will inform everything they do each day.

Second, institutional leaders must own and lead the diversity work. They must be institutional diversity champions, and to do so they must be knowledgeable about issues of diversity and inclusion and develop the skills necessary to infuse and embed a diversity mind-set into their current responsibilities. Students quite correctly often see themselves as the primary innovators on campus. However, long-term systemic change requires a time commitment that goes beyond the typical four-year tenure of a student. Institutional leadership, faculty, and senior administrators must provide the leadership for sustained diversity work.

We have also taken an evidence-based approach to our work. What we have learned from careful study of other institutions, the literature,[2] and most importantly, from the experience of our students, faculty, and staff has provided a solid evidence base for planning and action.

Though initially led and continuously championed by the leadership team, our diversity journey has depended upon significant cooperation and cross-fertilization of ideas among many on campus, including academic affairs, student development, admission, advancement, the board of trustees, and more. The call to enhance the overall student experience has resulted in new intersections among various campus constituencies, as faculty, administrators, and staff (collectively and individually) make sense of students' Kalamazoo experience.

Once the board of trustees endorsed the strategic plan, our D&I work took on greater depth and breadth, including requirements for accountability. Combined with our infuse-and-embed philosophy, our work developed in some thematic ways.

Themes

Representational Diversity

Though not sufficient in itself, a necessary step in creating a more inclusive campus community is addressing representational diversity—that is, the makeup of the student body, faculty, staff, trustees, and alumni board. At Kalamazoo, we took several explicit steps to enhance our representational diversity.

- The admissions office restructured staffing, travel, and recruitment strategies specifically to increase the number of students of color, international students, and students from outside Michigan, and to enhance the socioeconomic diversity of the student body.
- Although the staff already included a coordinator of multicultural recruitment, every member of the admission staff was given responsibility for the recruitment of underrepresented students. All admission counselors are expected to establish ties with high-performing, inner-city high schools and with community-based organizations (CBOs), such as LINK Unlimited and College Possible.
- Guidance counselors from these schools and CBOs are routinely invited to Kalamazoo's campus for an introduction to the college and for meaningful discussion on the topic of advising students of color for college admission.
- An annual multicultural student fly-in program provides high-achieving, underrepresented students with an early exposure to the campus.
- The advancement staff works with alumni and friends of the college to increase financial resources to support scholarships. This included a

gift to fund a five-year partnership with the Posse Foundation starting in 2009–2010, which provided a major boost to our efforts to create a more diverse student body.

- The college has made less significant strides on faculty and staff diversity, although this remains an important priority. The provost has more explicitly engaged faculty search committees in crafting position descriptions and building and assessing the qualifications of a more diverse pool of applicants. More recently, the office of human resources has made changes in recruiting strategies for staff positions, creating targeted job postings that might engage more diverse populations, and emphasizing building diverse candidate pools. The college has also taken advantage of opportunity hires as a way to build the diversity of the employee base.

We have seen tremendous success in enhancing the representational diversity of the student body. From fall 2005 to fall 2014, the student body has changed from 9.8% domestic students of color to 26.0%, from 0.4% degree-seeking international students to 6.4%, and from 8.9% Pell-eligible students to 21.7%.

Capacity Building

Another important theme in our work over the past decade was explicit attention to building capacity for diversity and inclusion across all members of the campus community, understanding that intersections across divisions and job classifications would enhance our success. After a team of faculty and staff attended the spring 2008 Diversity Summit sponsored by the Great Lakes Colleges Association, Kalamazoo prioritized building the capacity of the employee base and identified VISIONS, Inc., as consultants and one of our key partners for this part of our work.

This capacity-building work started with the president's staff, all of whom participated in the first VISIONS workshop in 2009. The leadership team subsequently engaged in a yearlong process of ongoing learning and discussion as follow-up. Most of the team has participated in a second, more advanced workshop, and they continue to meet with the VISIONS consultants to focus on how best to continue advancing diversity and inclusion initiatives on campus.

The VISIONS workshops have been a key strategy for continued capacity building among faculty and staff. To date, 56% of employees have participated. The college has also supported other diversity and inclusion initiatives for faculty, staff, and students. This has included trainings through

Eliminating Racism and Claiming/Celebrating Equality (ERAC/CE), a local group that focuses on building antiracist organizations; a minigrant program to which employees can apply and in which they can create opportunities to further enhance our capacity for this work; and dedicated time at new-employee orientation for discussing the institution's commitment to and work on diversity and inclusion.

Evidence-Based Focus

Throughout our work, we have given sustained attention to the quality of the student experience and considered real ways we could improve it. One of the best tools we employed was campus-based research, which informed our planning and action. Here, we recount some specific examples.

The vice president for student development and the provost collaborated to create a cross-divisional "data and decisions" group in 2008–2009. The group's first project was analysis of existing data (primarily through the National Survey of Student Engagement and the Higher Education Research Institute's Cooperative Institutional Research Program surveys) on students' expectations for and experiences with diversity. A significant early finding from this group was that Kalamazoo students, across the board, came to campus with higher expectations for experiences with diversity than students at peer institutions, that their expectations "were not met" at higher rates than students at peer institutions, and that our student athletes were more satisfied with their experiences with diversity than the Kalamazoo student body in general. This was followed by a focus-group research project to better understand the experiences of African American students. These findings, which were echoed in subsequent focus-group research, helped us understand that students experienced the campus differently based on their racial identity (e.g., extra scrutiny for students of color, the expectation that such students "represent" all other students of color), that the capacity of the overall community to fully engage with issues of difference was limited in ways that negatively impacted students (both in the classroom and with peers outside of the classroom), and that there were real actions that could mitigate the negative experiences of our African American students.

Several years later an expanded set of focus groups examined the diversity-related experiences of a wide range of students (i.e., what were students' direct experiences encountering diversity on campus—intentionally and unintentionally, with peers, in the classroom, and outside the classroom). These focus groups led to a spring 2013 report entitled "In Their Own Words," the overall findings of which were presented to the entire campus. The following year, the president's staff charged a group of students, faculty, and staff with delving more deeply into the findings and recommending ways in which the college could respond. Their report, "We Too Are K'zoo," placed the findings in context by exploring how issues of race are playing out on other campuses across the United States and examining the extensive literature on diversity in academe. It also incorporated the experiences and perspectives of Kalamazoo faculty and staff and offered specific recommendations for moving forward. Some key recommendations included ongoing training for faculty and staff, broader curricular innovation and change focused on diversity and inclusion, recruitment of faculty and staff of color, enhanced support for international students, and consistent messaging about the college's commitment to and accountability for D&I-related competency. In response to "We Too Are K'Zoo," a variety of efforts are now underway. The "sense of belonging" construct (Strayhorn, 2012) identified in the report was widely adopted by the college and encouraged the formation of a foundation for a grant on diversity and inclusion now being funded by the Andrew W. Mellon Foundation. The activities of the grant represent another example of collaboration between academic affairs and student development and will support additional faculty and staff capacity building, address inclusion through curricular and pedagogical lenses, and provide additional support for inclusion work in student development.

Several years ago, we looked at the participation of three cohorts of graduates in what we designated "high-impact practices." Our analysis showed significant differences by gender (men's participation rates were generally lower) but no apparent or significant differences based on race. A trend of decreasing study abroad participation, a signature experience for most Kalamazoo students, prompted us to form focus groups with students who chose not to study abroad, and the results led to changes in our recruiting approach and the historical messaging of study abroad as the opportunity for intercultural experiences. This shift in message focus to include other important outcomes of study abroad is meant to enhance the participation numbers of international students and domestic students of color.

While much of our work has been informed by formal intersectional research and subsequent action, we have also taken action informed by opportunity or more tacit information. The following are some examples of such courses of action:

- From 2008 to 2010, the college received a grant from the Council of Independent Colleges and the Walmart Foundation to support general programming and summer internships for first-generation students. This opportunity jump-started what has turned into sustained programs in support of first-generation students, including an orientation brunch for students and their families and a formalized organization of first-generation students named G1. It also led us to look at issues of financial access to internships for all students.

- After a student conducted and shared his senior research project on the experiences of the growing Latin@ population on campus, we asked an emerita faculty member to spend the next year getting to know this student cohort better and to make recommendations for action.

- As the international student population grew, we recognized the need for more systemic support and a better understanding of relevant issues, and we established the International Student Issues Committee, which now meets quarterly.

- The increasing voice of transgender students on campus led to establishing gender-neutral bathrooms, updating the student housing policy, and developing practices that enable students to use preferred names and pronouns on campus.

- The office of religious and spiritual life has greatly expanded its support of a wide range of religious traditions, recruited a diverse group of student workers/volunteers, and developed a strong interfaith focus.

- Academic advisers and faculty members have learned more about working with neurodiverse students, such as those on the autism spectrum.

All of these efforts are examples of the intersectional nature of our work, in which various offices and student groups collaborate to make the campus more inclusive in a variety of ways.

Curriculum and Pedagogy

As an educational institution, Kalamazoo considers curriculum and pedagogy essential elements of D&I work. Perhaps the most significant change was the recent faculty approval of a new major, critical ethnic studies. While calls for area or ethnic studies at Kalamazoo date back to 1968, a student demonstration in fall 2012 helped launch the current initiative. The provost convened a working group of faculty to investigate the course and vision of ethnic studies at the college. The full faculty engaged in a discussion of the possibility of ethnic studies at Kalamazoo in late winter 2013. This groundwork led to a proposal to and grant from the Andrew W. Mellon Foundation (different from the one mentioned previously) that supported a two-year visiting faculty member in ethnic studies to work closely with faculty on issues of race, diversity, and inclusion in the curriculum generally and to work with a core faculty group to develop a proposed ethnic studies curriculum. In late fall 2014 the faculty approved this new major.

Beyond this specific curriculum development initiative, the faculty has devoted its attention to a wide spectrum of diversity and inclusion issues in many venues. These include our annual fall colloquia, which have brought to campus over the years scholars and thought leaders like Freeman Hrabowski, III, Beverly Daniel Tatum, and Saundra McGuire. Teaching and learning workshops have engaged faculty in considering how their pedagogies, their curricular content, and even their reading lists do or do not foster inclusive diversity. For example, some faculty members have changed the way small groups are constructed in their courses to ensure that no students are excluded in an inadvertent way, something consistently cited by students who participated in focus-group research.

We see our work toward diversity and inclusion at Kalamazoo as ongoing, without an obvious end in sight. We have learned a great deal on our journey to date and offer some of the lessons we have learned.

Lessons Learned

The infuse-and-embed philosophy may at times be in direct conflict with symbolic action that may satisfy or placate the immediate demands of the community. For example, as a result of our approach, we opted not to appoint a chief diversity officer. Instead, the college has provided ongoing professional development to enable members of the executive team to lead the work within their units. When vacancies in the leadership team occurred, the capacity to lead and/or contribute significantly to institutional diversity efforts represented an important lens used to screen candidates. For some, the absence of a diversity officer signals a lack of commitment rather than an executive team that was taking full ownership of its responsibility.

Change of this type and magnitude takes a long time. It is hard work, and it does not always progress in a straight line. For example, Kalamazoo's success in increasing representational diversity in a short time frame led to increased and sometimes heated demands for further change (e.g., regular demonstrations demanding an ethnic studies curriculum as well as a dedicated intercultural center) by domestic students of color and others. Increasing the diversity of the community and building awareness of related issues do not "solve" the challenges of D&I. They complicate the issues in necessary, growth-producing ways that are sometimes hard and unpleasant.

It is helpful to normalize the "bumpiness" that comes with serious attention to D&I. We recognize the value of setting and communicating reasonable expectations about the time involved in culture change (always slower than we want it to be and never finished) and of continually cultivating empathy on a community-wide basis as a primary condition for changing together.

It is important to acknowledge and continuously reinforce the complexity of this work, while simultaneously keeping the community apprised of progress. An individual or a team can be so deeply engaged in the work that it is assumed that everyone else can see what is being done. Communication on diversity efforts and outcomes should occur often and in multiple formats. Lessons learned should be shared broadly and often so that the community understands what is being learned and so that past diversity work can inform future efforts.

It is extremely important to provide support and encouragement to all on campus as they attempt to recognize and interact with people in new ways that might challenge deep-seated values and habits. The effort to change will not be without mistakes. To initiate and sustain long-term cultural change, everyone must cultivate a generosity of spirit and an openness that allow for the collective exploration and examination of mistakes in a spirit of learning. Getting others across campus to take ownership of this work also takes time, and it can come with anger or frustration with senior leadership. Recent examples of this type of ownership taking include Sister Circle, a support group for women of color provided through the counseling center; employees organizing their own follow-up to VISIONS or ERAC/CE training; and regular self-organized gatherings of faculty of color.

We also learned that comprehensive leadership and resources matter. We have already addressed some aspects of leadership. As another example, sustaining the college's involvement in the Posse Scholars program at the end of its onetime, five-year grant required that the board of trustees take charge and include this significant financial commitment to increasing representational diversity in the operational budget. We translated strategic actions for D&I work into campaign priorities (e.g., scholarship endowments) and have sought and received grants to support our work from foundations and individuals.

Starting serious D&I work is challenging; continuing it is even more challenging in some ways because progress can be difficult to gauge. As the capacity and awareness of the institution are developed, more problematic practices, habits, and artifacts are discovered which, ideally, should lead to change. However, long-term, "taken-for-granted" institutional practices can be very difficult to change once the need is identified. This is more subtle work than recruiting a diverse student body, and it is not easy.

We look forward to the next chapter of Kalamazoo's work in creating a diverse and inclusive student-focused campus. And we hope the information shared in this chapter about our approach and the lessons learned will help others as they work on diversity and inclusion within their own contexts.

Notes

1. Communication from the Inclusivity Audit report reproduced in this chapter has remained anonymous and identified with "personal communication."

2. Among the literature we reviewed, we found the following particularly helpful: Gusa (2010), who wrote about the culture of Whiteness within predominantly White institutions; Strayhorn (2012), who discussed students' sense of belonging; and various publications from the American Association of Colleges and Universities on diversity, equity, and inclusion.

References

Gusa, D. L. (2010). White institutional presence: The impact of Whiteness on campus climate. *Harvard Educational Review, 80*(4), 464–490.

Schneider, K. (2003). *Michigan apartheid: Reforming land use policy can help most segregated state*. Retrieved from http://www.mlui.org/mlui/news-views/articles-from-1995-to-2012.html?archive_id=204#.VdUB3LJViko

Strayhorn, T. L. (2012). *College students' sense of belonging: A key to educational success for all students*. New York, NY: Routledge.

PART TWO

ENVIRONMENT

6

STRIVING FOR AN INCLUSIVE AND NURTURING CAMPUS

Cultivating the Intersections

Jon Dooley and Lucy LePeau

Imagine that your institution has accepted an invitation to be part of a national initiative for strengthening diversity and inclusion in higher education and has received a grant to support this effort. Although your campus has made strides in recent years, faculty, staff, and students agree there is significant room for improvement. The representational demographic diversity of the campus has increased, but many members of the campus community (students, faculty, and staff alike) still report feeling marginalized and are concerned about decision making at the institution and whether the commitment to diversity and inclusion is genuine. The curriculum has benefitted from previous diversity infusion projects, but in a recent campus climate study, many respondents noted the absence of particular perspectives and voices in the curriculum. And where concerns have traditionally been centered on racial diversity within the curriculum, increasingly the questions have become about multiple perspectives, identities, and histories: race, gender and gender expression, sexual orientation, political affiliation, national origin, disability, socioeconomic status, and so on. Campus curriculum committees and the academic senate were already raising the issue of diversity within the curriculum prior to the institution's acceptance into the cohort for the national diversity and inclusion initiative. Campus life has been another area of concern. Even as the campus has become more diverse, climate surveys suggest that students do not interact with individuals different from themselves (race, religion, political orientation, socioeconomic status) at higher rates. Students with both dominant and nondominant identities describe a campus climate that does not feel inclusive or supportive of diversity. Students also assert that they are consulted in regard to campus decision making but are shielded from the politics that take place behind closed doors. Similarly, staff and faculty with marginalized identities at the institution are predominantly younger and in positions with limited power and influence, reporting that leadership decisions affecting campus climate happen "to them" rather than "with them." Some faculty and staff have pointed out that every few years an incident on campus brings attention to the issue, protests take place, and promises and proclamations are made, but progress has seemed slow. Many campus constituencies are also challenging the institution to focus on multiple forms of identity in the cocurricular experience, raising concerns that the resources of the multicultural center in the division of student affairs are limited and focused primarily on race. In this context, you are excited to be part of the high-profile initiative for diversity and inclusion. The announcement of the initiative and grant in Washington, DC, was well publicized and resulted in enthusiasm on campus, in the community, and among alumni. The new effort is ready to commence. How will you engage the complex work of cultivating an inclusive campus for all members of the campus community (students, faculty, and staff), with a particular focus on intersectionality and multiple forms of identity?

Although this vignette is hypothetical, the central challenges it presents are common among postsecondary institutions of all types across the country. In spite of decades of initiatives focused on diversity (e.g., valuing and learning across differences related to identities such as religion, culture, and race) and inclusion (e.g., identifying how privilege and evolving oppressions influence experiences of campus educators in different environments; enacting programs, policies, and practices aimed at dismantling systematic marginalization; and doing ongoing reflective work in this process of creating welcoming environments), many individuals and institutions are dissatisfied with the progress made on their campuses. The vignette describes what have become two central components of that environment—the "curricular" or in-class setting and the "cocurricular" or out-of-class experience. While these contexts may be separate structurally, most students do not experience higher education as solely one or the other, and their learning transcends these boundaries of campus organization and environment. Further, *campus educators,* a term we use to include both faculty and staff, often want to bridge these organizational divides. In this chapter, we address intersectionality in the campus environment, in terms both of multiple forms of individual identity and organizational culture and how multiple areas of the campus come together to address diversity and inclusion. After describing these key contexts, we highlight pathways for effective campus partnerships to support diversity and inclusion and offer recommendations for establishing and nurturing effective partnerships that improve campus environments.

Intersectionality and Multiple Forms of Identity

Identity is not developed or understood in isolation. Systems of power, privilege, and oppression in society shape how an individual experiences and makes meaning of intersecting identities in different environments. Intersectionality addresses multiple interlocking systems of oppression rather than examining inequities solely through a singular lens, such as sexism, racism, or classism (Crenshaw, 1991; Nash, 2008). Specifically, Crenshaw's (1991) legal study explained that women of color who experience domestic violence are oppressed in ways that antiracism and feminism fail to address. The structure of the law forced women to describe their injuries in terms of either their race or their gender rather than addressing both forms of discrimination simultaneously (Crenshaw, 1991; Nash, 2008). Crenshaw (1991) illuminated gaps in the legal system that reinforced an essentialist view of identity: "Because women of color experience racism in ways not always the same as those experienced by men of color and sexism in ways not always parallel to White women, antifeminism and feminism are limited, even on their own terms" (p. 1252). Despite the value of that insight, debates continue about what intersectionality is, who is intersectional, and how to thoughtfully employ intersectionality as a methodology to inform policies and practices in higher education (Mitchell, 2014; Nash, 2008; Wijeyesinghe & Jones, 2014).

Abes, Jones, and McEwen (2007) provided a useful model for understanding how intersectionality and multiple dimensions of identity are influenced by an individual's environment, the individual's capacity for making meaning and filtering out contextual influences, and the individual's understanding of his or her own identities, as well as by the salience of particular aspects of those identities in varying environmental contexts. As in an earlier version of the model (Jones & McEwen, 2000), they suggested that a core sense of self (personal attributes, characteristics, and identity) is surrounded by dimensions of identity, such as race, gender, sexual orientation, social class, religion, and so on. They acknowledged that identity is understood and experienced within the context of family background, sociocultural conditions, current experiences, career decisions, and life planning. This context plays a role in the fluidity and salience of particular dimensions of identity associated with an individual's core sense of self (Abes et al., 2007; Jones & McEwen, 2000). The later version of this model introduced the concept of a meaning-making filter that individuals possess, with varying degrees of complexity. An individual with a more complex, "foundational" meaning-making filter is less influenced by contextual influences, such as peers, family, norms, and stereotypes, than an individual with a less complex, "transitional" or "formulaic" meaning-making capacity (Abes et al., 2007).

When considering environmental influences on intersectionality and student identity, it is important to consider not only the campus environment, but also students' identity development—both their self-perceptions and their developmental capacity to understand and filter the messages they receive from the context of their environment. Students' experiences at colleges and universities are often interpreted and understood through the lens of a single aspect of their identity (e.g., race, gender, disability, social class) without regard to other aspects of identity or to the salience that dimension of identity has for the student.

In the vignette presented at the beginning of the chapter, these tensions are emerging as students challenge the institution to focus diversity efforts on multiple perspectives, identities, and histories and, in doing so, demand that the institution more explicitly address the identities that individuals are finding most salient in their lived experience in the campus environment. Singling out individual aspects of identity for research and assessment may provide clarity and can assist in identifying challenges related to campus climate, but ignoring the complexities of salience and intersectionality may also contribute to "oppression Olympics," whereby two or more groups are examined to determine which is more oppressed. When campus educators foreground intersectionality in research or practice, they should emphasize the experiences of marginalized groups and avoid reinforcing the experiences of individuals and groups with privileged identities and further oppressing those with marginalized identities (Wijeyesinghe & Jones, 2014). Campus educators, in both academic affairs and student affairs, should deconstruct how particular institutional policies, programs, and practices are designed, for whose benefit, and why.

Campus Environments That Support Diversity and Inclusion

Several researchers have described how examining multiple aspects of campus climate is a crucial part of understanding environments that support diversity and inclusion (Hurtado, Milem, Clayton-Pedersen, & Allen, 1999; Milem, Chang, & Antonio, 2005; Williams, Berger, & McClendon, 2005). Recently, Hurtado, Alvarez, Guilllermo-Wann, Cuellar, and Arellano (2012) built upon the work of previous scholars in developing the multicontextual model for diverse learning environments (DLE model), which acknowledges the multiple contexts that influence higher education institutions (sociohistorical context, policy context, community context, and external commitments) and the importance of the institutional climate for diversity (historical, organizational, computational, psychological, and behavioral) as they shape individual student processes, outcomes, and successes. The DLE model accounts for intersectionality and multiple forms of identity and places the teaching and learning that occurs within an institution at the center of the model. Curricular and cocurricular contexts are described as parallel but separate processes that influence student outcomes and success based on such factors as "who we teach (student identities), who teaches (instructor identities), what is taught (content), and how it is taught (pedagogies/teaching methods)" (Hurtado et al., 2012, p. 49). Unfortunately, in describing learning environments as either curricular or cocurricular, Hurtado and colleagues relied on a classic division between "classroom" and "out-of-class" learning that suggests that the campus environment for diversity and inclusion is experienced in isolated contexts, rather than in a web or network of campus experiences that influence each other and work together in more complex ways.

At many institutions, particularly four-year colleges and universities and/or those with a strong residential component, the divisions between curricular and cocurricular aspects of campus life can be pronounced. Arcelus (2011) suggested that these divisions between curricular and cocurricular approaches can be traced back to an earlier debate about the nature of undergraduate education and theories and approaches espoused by John Dewey (1938) and Robert Hutchins (1936). Arcelus indicated that Dewey's focus on meaning making, experiential learning, and a constructivist approach to education can be viewed as most congruent with cocurricular learning environments and provides a philosophical basis for the work of student affairs educators and academic administrators. By contrast, the writings of Hutchins emphasize intellectual inquiry and a liberal arts education that provides a common academic core curriculum focused on reading and discussing great books in the Western tradition, engrossing students in the life of the mind. Arcelus suggested that Hutchins's approach undergirds the perspectives that many faculty hold today, with a particular focus on curricular learning. The debate continues, according to Arcelus (2011), and contributes, in part, to a "fragmented and competitive campus" (p. 67), where faculty and student affairs staff vie for resources, centrality to the institutional mission, and students' time and attention. In this context, academic primacy and the life of the mind compete with the education of the whole person, even though it is quite possible that all campus educators can exemplify commitment to the whole person.

Thus, partnerships between academic affairs and student affairs can help campus educators determine where gaps and inequities in educating the whole student exist on campus and identify where organizational policies, practices, and procedures reinforce competition between academic affairs and student affairs at the expense of student success and learning. It is critical, therefore, to consider the value of intersectionality in relation to the ways faculty, students, and staff occupying multiple social locations perceive campus environments and the ways campus environments affirm and/or oppress intersecting identities of faculty, staff, and students. Partnerships also challenge faculty and student affairs practitioners to face stereotypes they may have about each other and their respective cultures.

When addressing situations similar to the case example provided by the vignette, careful consideration must be given to the nature of partnerships and who is "at the table" when launching initiatives for diversity and inclusion. Campus educators must demonstrate a shared responsibility and commitment to the ongoing work necessary to create welcoming and inclusive environments for students (Arminio, Torres, & Pope, 2012; Clayton-Pedersen, Parker, Smith, Moreno, & Teraguchi, 2007; Hurtado et al., 2012; Milem et al., 2005; Williams, et al., 2005). Structures within institutions often privilege or marginalize particular campus stakeholders—for example, by situating influence and campus leadership with the faculty and leaving students and staff at the margins. When inequities are left unexamined and unaltered, systems that oppress faculty, staff, and students in campus environments remain firmly intact. Because every institution is different, campus educators need to attend to the specific context of the institution when designing robust diversity and inclusion initiatives.

Effective Partnerships for Diversity and Inclusion

In an examination of partnerships for diversity and inclusion between academic affairs and student affairs areas, LePeau (2015a) found three variations of the partnerships that served as an important pathway to successful implementation of diversity and inclusion initiatives. In a *complementary pathway*, academic affairs and student affairs professionals worked separately within their respective divisions to advance diversity and inclusion. Although such work is complementary, it does not require individuals to address cultural contradictions between the areas. For example, individuals in academic affairs address changes to the general education curriculum, while those in student affairs address programs in the residence halls that examine issues of race, class, and gender. In a *coordinated pathway*, the partnership between academic affairs and student affairs is marked by a shared vision for diversity and inclusion, professionals who assume hybrid roles between the two divisions, campus committees that lead to communication across units, and a recognition of the cultural contradictions of one division having more power and influence than the other. In a *pervasive pathway*, partnerships between academic affairs and student affairs are the campus norm, grounded in the understanding that individuals in both units are considered educators on the campus. As they support diversity and inclusion initiatives, individuals from these two units work from a shared vision, rethink classroom pedagogy and cocurricular programming to consciously address social identity, blur the organizational boundaries between academic affairs and student affairs, challenge cultural contradictions between the two divisions, consider shared governance, and make partnerships between academic affairs and student affairs the standard operating culture on campus. Faculty and student affairs practitioners accomplish initiatives in every type of partnership; however, the most transformative type is the pervasive pathway, because it is the one in which faculty and student affairs practitioners alter inequities in organizational policies and practices.

The cultivation of effective campus partnerships to support an inclusive campus climate for all students, faculty, and staff requires intentional focus and commitment. Grounded in previous research on effective partnerships (LePeau, 2015a, 2015b), the six recommendations presented here are designed to help individuals and campus groups navigate the complex work required to address diversity and inclusion in the campus partnership.

Recognize Your Own Identities and Intersections

Case studies of diversity in higher education often challenge readers to consider multiple approaches as they reflect on how they would respond to complex situations. Weigand and LePeau (2012) encouraged case study respondents addressing issues of diversity and inclusion to also foreground their own identity as they formulated their responses. Faculty and administrators who are working together to shape and influence campus climate cannot ignore that they are shaped simultaneously by that current environment, their previous environments, and the multiple forms of their own identity (oppressed and privileged) that are salient to themselves and to those with whom they interact. Taking time to carefully reflect on one's own identity and intersections in the context of establishing effective partnerships contributes to authentic interactions and an appreciation for the complexities of intersectionality. In responding to the situation presented by the introductory vignette, for example, it would be important for each of the individuals involved in developing a campus initiative for diversity and inclusion to carefully consider their own multiple forms of identity, how they relate to the campus environment and challenges presented, and how they take on different forms of salience and intersection with the multiple identities of other individuals involved in responding. In a coordinated pathway, student affairs and academic affairs leaders appointed to committees could infuse practices such as: incorporating readings to engender ongoing professional development and reflection about how positionalities of committee members inform the work, changing facilitator roles during meetings to bring in different voices, and providing opportunities for both written and oral feedback about the process to be gathered by committee chairs. The ongoing reflection required to bring identity, power, and privilege to the surface in complex situations like the one presented by the vignette requires substantial time and energy if effective partnerships are to be established. This work is difficult and requires campus educators to build in time during day-to-day work and committee meetings to regularly consider how their identities influence practice, rather than relegating such considerations to retreats and trainings. These conversations may unearth how practices may reinforce (even if unintentionally) dominant cultures in campus environments.

Examine Who Creates and Is Charged to Implement Inclusion Initiatives

Students do not experience campus environments in isolated silos that mirror organizational charts for educational institutions. Likewise, learning occurs across environmental contexts, inside the classroom and beyond. Effective partnerships that holistically address diversity and inclusion across the campus begin with goals that are designed collectively, with a broad representation of campus constituents coming together. In the spirit of the adage "people support what they help create," such coalitions, including both academic affairs and student affairs educators, lead to commitment to diversity and inclusion across multiple contexts throughout the campus and help move past the power differential and debates about the primacy of roles in colleges and universities. The vignette illustrates that challenges related to diversity and inclusion are not experienced in an isolated part of the campus environment (curricular or cocurricular) and that, therefore, an effective response necessarily includes individuals from across the campus working together collaboratively, in careful coordination. Leadership for the initiative must similarly transcend traditional boundaries. For example, if faculty create annual reports that go only to the provost, and student affairs professionals generate annual reports that go to the chief student affairs officer (sometimes reporting to the provost and sometimes not), there are too many opportunities for duplication of efforts without any coordination.

This practice is typical of an institution operating in a complementary pathway. The people in positional leadership need to not only know about what initiatives have been accomplished, but also consider ways to bring together diverse resources (e.g., financial and personnel) as they shift toward more systematic approaches.

Furthermore, when positional leaders, such as deans, vice presidents, provosts, and presidents, formulate committees or work groups, they should critically examine the composition of the teams. Leaders might consider the number of faculty and staff employed at the institution and consider whether committee members are representative of the proportion of faculty and staff from both academic affairs and student affairs departments. For example, if a committee has a faculty representative from every academic unit, but only one or two student affairs staff and one or two students, the composition may reflect an imbalance in structural and power dynamics that will be an impediment for the work of the group.

For example, a campus on a complementary pathway might respond to the situation outlined in the vignette using a multiple-committee approach, with separate teams of student affairs staff and academic affairs faculty and staff working on initiatives within their purview, with a careful understanding of what each group is working on and responsible for. In a coordinated pathway, those two groups might be subcommittees of a unified structure (with proportional representation of educators from both groups), led by individuals who have developed strong relationships and reputations as "boundary crossers." To address the issues presented in the vignette in the spirit of a pervasive pathway, the idea of a campus team with individuals from different areas of campus would not be an anomaly, but would be standard operating practice and an expectation of the campus leadership. In this spirit, a blended team of students, faculty, and staff would work collectively and collaboratively to identify and address the multiple issues, questions, possibilities, and opportunities presented by the complex set of circumstances. These teams may create spaces for campus educators and students to take a multidimensional approach to inclusion efforts, because people are not charged to make suggestions solely based on a singular role or identity (i.e., faculty focused only on curriculum, students focused on representing their respective club or organization) but rather to look at the institution as a web, as in the DLE model. These spaces may also provide an opportunity to address questions about how interlocking systems of oppression arise (e.g., ethnocentrism, sexism, trans*phobia, religious intolerance) in the environment from an intersectional rather than a singular-identity standpoint.

Cultivate Relationships With Campus Constituents

Campus committees or working groups established to address diversity and inclusion are often responding to incidents of concern, or institutional priorities linked to dissatisfaction with the current situation. Such work typically feels urgent, creating pressure to recommend and implement solutions quickly. But addressing the complexity of intersectionality and working across campus contexts requires substantial time and effort to nurture authentic relationships that have the capacity to enable individuals and teams to effectively address diversity and inclusion. Campus working groups that comprise a broad representation of campus constituents can also immerse groups of individuals who do not normally work together in complex collaborative work. These relationships can be difficult to form when constituents have experienced bias and oppression on campus. The vignette provides examples of the mistrust and disappointment related to prior efforts that require careful attention as a team is assembled for a new initiative. Effective relationships in this context should be established and cultivated in a deliberate fashion, building capacity before incidents happen.

Each of the authors has served on successful campus committees where care, focus, and attention were given to relationships and members of the group were expected to invest the time required to address issues of power, privilege, and oppression within the campus environment and the committee itself. Likewise, we have each experienced working groups and campus environments where mistrust was bred by a lack of transparency, unrecognized privilege, unhealthy power dynamics, and a lack of commitment on the part of key stakeholders to invest time in developing productive relationships. Unsurprisingly, the ability of the committees or groups to effect positive change in the campus environment was a direct reflection of the quality of the relationships among the individuals and departments expected to address diversity and inclusion on campus. All campus educators, regardless of the pathway from which they operate, need to attend to cultivating relationships.

Actively Engage Students as Partners

Relationships and partnerships for advancing campus diversity and inclusion efforts should not be exclusive to faculty and staff. Any truly inclusive response to the challenges of shaping culture requires the contributions of all members of the campus community, including students as partners and leaders. Initiatives often take place over a number of years; the sustained work required can sometimes present barriers to student participation (not the least of which is how and when to schedule meetings). And yet students can be the most effective agents in shaping and influencing campus culture; their contributions should be considered essential to a successful effort.

Harnessing the power of student contributions requires identifying strategies for students to engage in meaningful roles, listening carefully to student voices about solutions they recommend for challenges they perceive in the campus climate, viewing students as partners in campus leadership, and cultivating future student leadership and engagement in diversity and inclusion initiatives. Moreover, students may unearth issues of marginalization absent from strategic plans and grant-supported campus-wide initiatives. Campus educators are challenged to join students (when students desire) or work with students to figure out how to mobilize their own efforts in building more inclusive environments rather than looking for students to support administration-driven initiatives.

In view of the tremendous diversity of student perspectives, caution should also be taken to avoid asking a handful of students to serve as "representatives" for all student perspectives or expecting students to participate in a way that reinforces binaries in identities or unintentionally makes them choose between identities. Instead, structures should be designed to maximize the inclusion of a diverse range of student perspectives in campus decision-making processes and working groups. Students should be invited and encouraged to offer insights about intersectionality that faculty and administrators may miss. One strategy might include the implementation of regular, comprehensive campus climate studies, which often take the form of campus educators conducting campus-wide surveys and subsequent focus groups. A strategy that includes the comprehensive and systematic collection of student input can not only ensure that a range of perspectives is heard and acted upon, but also encourage a more nuanced understanding of student perspectives that can account for intersectionality. Another strategy might be to include an additional intentional feedback loop before final recommendations or decisions are made, which invites students to present important considerations or describe forms of intersectionality that may have been overlooked in the process. Addressing the complexity of multiple and intersecting forms of identity requires that the inclusion of student voices in diversity and inclusion efforts is systematic, ongoing, and situated at multiple levels of the institutional structure. An institution that uses these comprehensive strategies may shift toward standard operating practices found in a pervasive pathway. Furthermore, through the adoption of processes that encourage greater administrative transparency, these proposed strategies may address the concern expressed by students and staff in the vignette about initiatives happening "to them" rather than "with them."

Seek Out Internal and External Mechanisms to Assess Institutional Efforts

The vignette exemplifies how policy makers, national associations, and foundations sponsor grant-funded programs for colleges and universities with the hopes of catalyzing deep and systemic institutional change. These initiatives can be powerful, because campus constituents can learn from researchers and practitioners at similar and different institutions about how they engage in addressing oppression and creating a welcoming campus climate (LePeau, 2015a). Campus constituents are often charged with writing project reports to chronicle their progress toward meeting their intended learning outcomes. What happens when learning outcomes are *not* met? How are institutions holding themselves accountable to continue the work once the grant-funded project ends? It is not enough to rehash strategic planning documents or redefine institutional mission statements to reflect appreciation for diversity. Institutions need to readminister campus climate surveys, conduct assessments to understand students' experiences in multiple environments (beyond satisfaction surveys and course evaluations), and teach students to integrate climate assessments into the ways they organize and lead clubs and groups. Campus educators must ensure that assessment results are critically analyzed, publicly communicated, and acted upon. A simple Google search for "assessment of campus climate for diversity" yields multiple examples of campuses that are boldly choosing to be transparent about their self-examination and are inviting members of their own campus community (not to mention public stakeholders beyond the campus) to hold them accountable to measuring, reporting, and responding to progress with diversity and inclusion efforts.

Transform Organization Structures and Systems

Effective pathways and partnerships for diversity and inclusion often necessitate addressing any divisions or barriers (perceived and real) between academic affairs and student affairs on college and university campuses (LePeau, 2015a, 2015b). This can happen through informal actions that encourage individuals to work beyond their particular departmental or functional area context, or it can be more formally encouraged by creating new organizational structures that bring together educators from multiple areas of the campus into new units or new relationships. For example, campuses can establish new departments, institutes, or centers that address academic and cocurricular campus contexts simultaneously and are staffed by individuals with nontraditional position descriptions, or they can create new opportunities for faculty and staff to come together as coeducators in campus learning experiences (classes, certificate programs, study abroad programs, service and immersion programs, or other engaged learning formats) that address diversity and inclusion. Innovation will look different from campus to campus, and should be responsive to the unique environment, context, and goals of the institution.

Conclusion

The chapter-opening vignette starts with campus educators naming and acknowledging barriers to building an inclusive campus environment. Because national grants or initiatives encourage institutional teams to make their efforts context-specific, the ideas presented in the vignette are merely hypothetical. When campus educators are doing ongoing work to create more inclusive environments, there are real faculty, students, and staff involved; each person possesses individual stories and lived experiences related to the inclusivity of campus environments. Thus, it is imperative to acknowledge the nuances missing from this vignette when applying this chapter's recommendations for enacting change in your own environment. The strengths of the people learning and working in your own institution need to be honored. Campus educators from different types of institutions (i.e., community college, minority-serving institution, Hispanic-serving institution, historically Black college or university, predominantly White institution, tribal college, religiously affiliated institution, liberal arts college, research university) in different regions of the country will view issues of inequity from their own positionalities and based on their own knowledge of the particular campus culture and climate. Campus educators who enter the work of forming intersections from an asset-based angle, where everyone is perceived as contributing to student success, have the potential to move beyond the rhetoric of valuing diversity and create ongoing change.

References

Abes, E. S., Jones, S. R., & McEwen, M. K. (2007). Reconceptualizing the model of multiple dimensions of identity: The role of meaning-making capacity in the construction of multiple identities. *Journal of College Student Development, 48*(1), 1–22.

Arcelus, V. J. (2011). Transforming our approach to education: Cultivating partnerships and dialogue. In P. M. Magolda & M. B. Baxter-Magolda (Eds.), *Contested issues in student affairs: Diverse perspectives and respectful dialogue* (pp. 61–73). Sterling, VA: Stylus.

Arminio, J. L., Torres, V., & Pope, R. L. (Eds.). (2012). *Why aren't we there yet? Taking personal responsibility for creating an inclusive environment.* Sterling, VA: Stylus.

Clayton-Pedersen, A. R., Parker, S., Smith, D. G., Moreno, J. F., & Teraguchi, D. H. (2007). *Making a real difference with diversity: A guide to institutional change.* Washington, DC: Association of American Colleges & Universities.

Crenshaw, K. (1991). Mapping the margins: Intersectionality, identity politics and violence against women in color. *Stanford Law Review, 43*(6), 1241–1299.

Dewey, J. (1938). *Experience and education.* New York, NY: Macmillan.

Hurtado, S., Alvarez, C. L., Guilllermo-Wann, C., Cuellar, M., & Arellano, L. (2012). A model for diverse learning environments: The scholarship on creating and assessing conditions for student success. In J. C. Smart & M. B. Paulsen (Eds.), *Higher education: Handbook of theory and research* (27th ed., pp. 41–122). New York, NY: Springer.

Hurtado, S., Milem, J., Clayton-Pedersen, A., & Allen, W. (1999). *Enacting diverse learning environments: Improving the climate for racial/ethnic diversity in higher education.* ASHE-ERIC Higher Education Report, *26*(8).

Hutchins, R. M. (1936). *The higher learning in America.* New Haven, CT: Yale University Press.

Jones, S. R., & McEwen, M. K. (2000). A conceptual model of multiple dimensions of identity. *Journal of College Student Development, 41*, 405–414.

LePeau, L. (2015a). A grounded theory of academic affairs and student affairs partnerships for diversity and inclusion aims. *Review of Higher Education. 39*(1), 97–122.

LePeau, L. A. (2015b). The transformational potential of academic affairs and student affairs partnerships for enacting multicultural initiatives. In S. Watt (Ed.). *Designing transformative multicultural initiatives* (pp. 180–190). Sterling, VA: Stylus.

Milem, J. F., Chang, M. J., & Antonio, A. L. (2005). *Making diversity work on campus: A research-based perspective.* Washington, DC: Association of American Colleges and Universities.

Mitchell, D. (Ed.). (2014). *Intersectionality and higher education: Theory, research, and praxis.* New York, NY: Peter Lang.

Nash, J. C. (2008). Re-thinking intersectionality. *Feminist Review, 89*, 1–15.

Weigand, M. J., & LePeau, L. A. (2012). Different approaches to real issues. In J. Arminio, V. Torres, & R. L. Pope (Eds.), *Why aren't we there yet? Taking personal responsibility for creating an inclusive campus* (pp. 145–186). Sterling, VA: Stylus.

Wijeyesinghe, C. L., & Jones, S. R. (2014). Intersectionality, identity, and systems of power and inequality. In D. Mitchell (Ed.), *Intersectionality and higher education: Theory, research, and praxis* (pp. 9–19). New York, NY: Peter Lang.

Williams, D. A., Berger, J. B., & McClendon, S. A. (2005). *Toward a model of inclusive excellence and change in postsecondary institutions.* Washington, DC: Association of American Colleges and Universities.

WHEN THINGS GO WRONG

Avoiding and Managing Collisions in the Intersections

Leigh-Anne Royster

Issues of bias, violence, and harassment erupt all too often on college and university campuses. When these incidents attract intense media attention, such as the racist fraternity chants at Oklahoma University or the *Rolling Stone* (Erdely, 2014) article about alleged rapes at the University of Virginia, many other campuses are forced to ask, "Could that happen here?"

Rather than waiting for an incident or a media firestorm to prompt action, higher education leaders should create robust approaches to prevent and respond to bias, violence, and harassment on campus. Because institutions are diverse, such policies and practices should reflect the particular dynamics of an institution and its community. The theory of intersectionality (Crenshaw, 1991; Hunt & Zajicek, 2008) emerged in part for this very purpose—to develop nuanced policies that recognize and honor the multiple aspects of identity in the face of oppressive acts, such as hate crimes (McPhail, 2002; Perry, 2001; Strolovitch, 2007). Intersectionality is also useful when developing policies and practices that aim to prevent or respond to acts of bias, violence, and harassment on campus.

Intersectionality suggests that systems of power should be understood as a constellation of mutually supporting power structures where each uses the others to reinforce the collective effect of the power and oppression (Collins, 2004; McCall, 2005). For example, many campuses pay more careful attention to certain parts of federal guidance related to Title IX than to other aspects of identity-based violence. Looking at this differential focus, we might ask ourselves: Are we willing to allocate resources only to protect against liability, or are we committed to supporting infrastructure that creates a welcoming and inclusive community that celebrates a wide variety of difference and lived experiences? One example of an intersectional policy that does not require extensive resource allocation is to include sexual orientation or gender identity as a protected category in a campus nondiscrimination statement.

This chapter highlights the importance of applying an intersectionality framework to acts of bias and harassment on a college campus to crafting effective policy and examining individual incidents of bias and harassment when they occur. While this chapter explores examples of specific incidents, fully developed prevention and response efforts must also take into account daily microaggressions and "othering" practices that occur on college campuses. It is important to include microaggressions in any analysis of bias and harassment on college campuses, as emerging literature has cited these daily acts as the cause for lower self-efficacy, frequent feelings of frustration, and in extreme instances, separation from the university for students who are the target of such acts (Solorzano & Yasso, 2000).

Campus Climate, Bias, and Intersectionality

Faculty, staff, and students' perceptions of diversity on a campus—whether structural-level diversity (e.g., campus environment) or availability of diversity-related activities—can impact their sense of integration and belonging, fostering more positive (or negative) interactions and social outcomes (Rankin & Reason, 2005; Umbach & Kuh, 2006). Research has indicated that institutions that lack strategies to improve interaction among all groups of students typically have a campus climate in which students spend most of their time within groups that represent their own identities. Without institutional action to promote cross-group interaction, students feel more comfortable with in-group interaction. This fragmented approach to interaction can result in increased harassment and physical violence toward marginalized groups of students (Meyer, 2004; Rankin, 2005; Stotzer & Hossellman, 2012).

Many studies have used surveys to examine differences in perceptions of campus climate related to respondents' race/ethnicity, gender, and sexual orientation (Maramba, 2008; Rankin & Reason, 2005; Reid & Radhakrishnan, 2003; Ryan, Broad, Walsh, & Nutter, 2013; Stotzer & Hossellman, 2012). In general, these studies demonstrate that harassment and violence, particularly toward minority groups, can have negative impacts on students' health; examples include alcohol and drug abuse, depression, post-traumatic stress disorder, and even suicide (D. Eisenberg, Downs, Golberstein, & Zivin, 2009; M. Eisenberg & Wechsler, 2003; Potter, Fountain, & Stapleton, 2012).

Examinations of identity-based bias and harassment have explored the particular incident(s) of aggression or the particular construct that caused the violence (e.g., racism, sexism, anti-Semitism). In addition, instances of identity-based bias or harassment are often boiled down to a particular identity construct (e.g., described as a racist incident or an act motivated by homophobia), when in reality, acts of bias or hate are typically more complex. Using an intersectional lens helps us tell a more contextualized story.

When we use an intersectional approach, a bias incident rarely appears to be adequately described by one construct, such as racism or homophobia, if we take into account the person's experience in the incident relative to his or her gender, faith tradition, class, age, and other salient aspects of total identity. Using an intersectional lens also helps us in prioritizing the agency of the targeted person. Only the person targeted is an authority on what the best response might be for him or her in the aftermath of an incident of bias or harassment.

In addition to the ways that intersectionality can help us frame our response and support of targeted individuals, it can help us create university processes and practices that provide the supporting framework for response and prevention efforts. Using an intersectional lens can help institutions in crafting the most comprehensive "menu" of options for individuals who have experienced bias. A philosophy that centers on a critical examination of the ways power and oppression operate allows for input about response from a myriad of offices, departments, and individuals. In the case of an incident of bias or hate, the targeted individual should have as much choice as possible in the steering of the response process. To make this kind of agency available to targeted people, an institution must engage and train numerous offices and individuals across campus.

The next section of this chapter explores specific incidents to highlight experiences of individuals at colleges and universities as they work through an intersectional lens in policy development and response. The examples shared in this chapter serve to illustrate how easy it is to abandon the agreed-upon philosophical underpinnings or framework when faced with criticism or unanticipated implications or incidents. Each example is based on actual campus incidents at private universities in the southern United States, but some details have been modified.

Composite Campus Example #1

Two first-year undergraduate women roommates returned to their residence hall one evening to find a swastika, a noose, and penises drawn on a piece of paper taped to the door of their room. One woman identified as Jewish and the other as African American. The students had positive social and academic experiences on campus until that point.

Shocked by these images, the Jewish student who lived in the room alerted friends in the large and well-organized Jewish student group on campus, including professional staff advisers. Students notified the national Hillel office, which contacted the campus to coordinate a response. The student who identified as African American, while upset, did not reach out as actively to peers or professionals on or off campus about the incident.

On many campuses, bias incidents like this often target more than one student, and those students often identify differently and have distinct expectations for institutional response. In this case, the campus community more actively responded to and cared for the student who was mobilizing the most energy. While university officials checked in with both students, the racial and gendered elements of this incident lost visibility. Consequently, one student received less support, and the campus missed opportunities to address the gender-based element and more fully explore the racist targeting of the incident.

Composite Campus Example #2

One morning, workers with environmental services were cleaning the student center on campus when they came across scores of fliers littering the floors and taped to walls. The fliers were half sheets of paper containing graphic racist, sexist, and homophobic slurs in large bold letters. At the top of each flier, in much smaller type, readers were invited to a campus event later that day to discuss the use of such language on campus. While student activists created the fliers to rally against acts of bias and hate on campus, the environmental services workers were shaken and concerned that individuals in their community would use such words.

In this instance, well-intentioned students had not considered the impact of their fliers on people beyond peers who already knew about the bias incidents under discussion. Nor did they consider how people from different generations, socioeconomic backgrounds, and campus roles might experience the fliers.

In this case, the campus missed an opportunity to reach out to the environmental service workers to offer support and to connect those employees with the students who created the fliers so they could understand each other's perspectives.

Case Study: Developing Campus-Wide Intersectional Policies

The following in-depth case study provides an example of how one institution, Elon University, attempted to maintain an intersectional approach in the policy-development processes around response to and prevention of incidents of bias, harassment, and violence.

A racist incident on campus prompted members of the Sexual Assault and Gender Issues Council (SAGIC) to rethink the scope of its ongoing examination of the university's sexual harassment policy. Accordingly, SAGIC evolved into a new group that included a variety of campus departments and constituencies that had oversight or a stake in issues of multiple forms of bias and harassment on campus.

Members of this broader group decided to use an intersectional and public health focus to develop a campus-wide policy that addressed all forms of identity-based bias, harassment, and violence. This framework accounted for the complex nature of identity-based bias and violence and ensured the addition of strong prevention and action strategies. The following steps outline the process the committee undertook to engage a diverse range of constituents and apply an intersectional lens to policy development.

Step 1: Engage All Invested Campus Parties in the Policy-Development Process

The committee expanded to include others from across campus, including student life, academics, human resources, business and finance, admissions, law enforcement, faculty with expertise in particular areas of identity development, and student representatives from cultural organizations. Participation from identity-based offices and the health promotion department ensured that the committee kept both the deep context of diverse identities and a prevention philosophy at the core of the policy-development process.

Step 2: Gather Input From the Community

The committee members held campus-wide forums, consulted individuals who had experienced bias, and talked with other campus and community offices. A critical step in this process was to invite input from many different perspectives, including those who sometimes do not have a significant voice in campus conversations, such as first-year students, groundskeepers, custodial staff, and adjunct faculty. The committee emphasized the importance of contributions from varied people and positions at the institution.

Step 3: Gather Input From Experts Outside the Community

The university hired an outside consultant to conduct interviews on campus and then to develop a report with recommendations. Because the consultant possessed significant expertise in this topic and experience working at a variety of institutions, the report brought additional perspectives and critical questions into the process.

Step 4: Build Consensus Around a Shared Policy and Protocol

Anyone who has attempted to build consensus around a complex set of recommendations may find this step daunting. It is critical, however, to have as many invested parties as possible when developing a campus-wide approach to something as sensitive and contentious as identity-based bias or violence. Concerns raised by any group should be taken seriously and weighed carefully as grounds for policy revision.

Results of This Four-Step Process

This four-step, inclusive process resulted in three broad outcomes: (a) an office to coordinate this work, (b) two new "teams" to work on education and on process, and (c) a revised approach to communicating with stakeholders about acts of bias, violence, and harassment on campus.

The new office (office of inclusive community well-being) houses one staff member. This member is the director, who oversees campus policies and practices related to bias and harassment, monitors and raises awareness about the reporting structures for identity-based bias and harassment, and delivers bias-prevention education. The director position was a new staff position funded in our budget process.

To complement the work of this office, the university also developed two new campus-wide groups: the education team and the process advocate team. The education team is made up of faculty, staff, and students from more than 25 disciplines and includes members with deep expertise in a variety of areas related to diversity and inclusion. The steering committee for this group is responsible for organizing "just in time" educational events in response to campus incidents or national debates related to issues of inequality. The team also organizes a campus-wide diversity roundtable series that is offered each semester for a required first-year core course. The roundtables introduce first-year students to key questions, concepts, and scholarship on diversity, power, and oppression.

Faculty and staff on the process advocate team embody a diverse array of identities and backgrounds. Members volunteer to serve in this capacity and undergo regular training regarding resources, processes, and options for targets of bias or harassment. Individuals reporting acts of bias can choose to be connected with someone from the process advocate team with whom they have already formed a relationship or with someone with whom they most closely identify. This is a critical step in honoring intersectionality by acknowledging in-group comfort and support in times of threat and by empowering the targeted person to choose who will be best able to serve as an advocate and ally.

While the office and these new teams have created more effective processes and supports, campus leaders still had to wrestle with vexing questions related to communicating about bias, violence, and harassment. During the policy-development process, many in the campus community expressed a desire to be made aware of incidents in their midst. However, others worried that sending out campus-wide notifications of every reported incident might actually harm the campus climate. Other community members expressed concern that public reporting beyond what is required by the Clery Act and Title IX might place the university at a competitive disadvantage when prospective students (or faculty and staff) compare Elon with peer institutions that adhere strictly to mandated reporting.

To balance these conflicting goals for transparency and maintaining a positive campus climate, university leaders developed a layered protocol for communicating campus incidents. When a bias report is received (either through the emergency response system or through the newly formed office), that information is immediately shared with the associate provost for inclusive community, the vice president for student life, the assistant vice president for student life (who oversees the emergency response system), and the director of the Office of Inclusive Community Well-Being. The director then shares the information with the offices on campus that most closely deal with any salient identity constructs. For instance, in Composite Campus Example #1, the director would have alerted professionals in offices related to race, religion, and gender.

Unless an immediate threat exists or the incident is already widely known, the entire campus community is not notified at this point. Instead, once each semester the director e-mails all students, faculty, and staff with a message that

- affirms the values of the institution;
- condemns acts of bias;
- explains the details of upcoming campus events where students, faculty, and staff can learn information about recent incidents on campus; and
- reminds the community about the reporting process and response options.

In the open forums that follow this e-mail, the director and others provide summaries of recent incidents, discuss any patterns that appear to exist, and answer questions. By offering aggregate information in face-to-face settings instead of alerting the campus each time an incident occurs, the communication process is transparent while remaining sensitive to the needs of both the target(s) of bias and the university.

Concluding Recommendations

To summarize, we offer a few best practices for the campus community.

Ensure Equity

In addressing bias and harassment on college campuses, faculty and staff responsible for developing policies and practices must create equitable responses to a diverse range of individuals and confront many types of bias. Institutions may have inequitable resources when it comes to supporting varying identities within their communities. However, with a campus-wide policy and practices that recognize intersectionality, institutions can come closer to developing equity among a diverse range of identities and communities and the offices and resources that support those communities. Through sharing resources, allowing equal access to policy-making spaces, inviting input across difference, and ensuring transparency of processes, institutions can create an effective and flexible intersectional approach to bias, violence, and harassment on campus.

Prioritize Choice and Agency for Targeted Individuals

A central understanding of the intersectionality framework is that our culture creates systems that keep interlocking oppressions in place; campus leaders should recognize the institution itself as one such system. Therefore, in an intersectional framework, colleges and universities must prioritize the agency of targeted individuals so they are not retraumatized by interactions with oppressive institutional practices in the aftermath of an incident of bias. For example, in Composite Campus Example #2, the environmental services workers should have access to skilled professionals who can help them make sense of this disturbing incident; their immediate supervisor may not have the experience necessary to offer that support, so the campus should tap others to assist these traumatized colleagues. Further, recognizing the potential intersectionality present in that example, the university's response should recognize the ways that different members of the environmental services staff might react to this experience. While the university should offer diverse resources, the individuals involved must have a voice in the process.

Focus Prevention on Education and Contextualization

The campus community as a whole benefits from a complex analysis of acts of bias and harassment and education that focuses on celebration of diversity. Therefore, key stakeholders should develop a campus-wide education plan that includes the following components:

- Anti-bias and violence-prevention education
- Bystander skill development
- Introductory cultural competency development
- Broad celebration and valuing of difference
- Educational "deeper dives" into specific aspects of creating inclusive communities

Additionally, offices should use a philosophy grounded in intersectionality to undergird that planning and implementation. Using an intersectionality framework supports better collaboration among offices that offer diversity education and can ensure engagement across difference within the campus community. It can provide the foundation for creating better systems through which to share resources and reduce the duplication of efforts. In this way, the intersectional frame becomes the cornerstone to prevention and response efforts regarding incidents of bias.

References

Choo, H. Y., & Ferree, M. M. (2010). Practicing intersectionality in sociological research: A critical analysis of inclusions, interactions, and institutions in the study of inequalities. *Sociological Theory, 28,* 129–149.

Collins, P. H. (2000). *Black feminist thought: Knowledge, consciousness and the politics of empowerment.* London, England: Routledge.

Collins, P. H. (2004). *Black sexual politics: African Americans, gender and the new racism.* London, England: Routledge.

Crenshaw, K. (1991). Mapping the margins: Intersectionality, identity politics, and violence against women of color. *Stanford Law Review, 43*(6), 1241–1299.

Eisenberg, D., Downs, M. F., Golberstein, E., & Zivin, K. (2009). Stigma and help seeking for mental health among college students. *Medical Care Research and Review, 66*(5), 522–541.

Eisenberg, M. E., & Wechsler, H. (2003). Social influences on substance-use behaviors of gay, lesbian, and bisexual college students: Findings from a national study. *Social Science & Medicine, 57*(10), 1913–1923.

Erdely, S. (2014, November 19). A rape on campus. *Rolling Stone.* Retrieved from http://web.archive.org/web/20141219172210/http://www.rollingstone.com/culture/features/a-rape-on-campus-20141119?page=7

Hancock, A.-M. (2007). When multiplication doesn't equal quick addition: Examining intersectionality as a research paradigm. *Perspectives on Politics, 5*(1), 63–79.

Hondagneu-Sotelo, P. (2001). *Domestica: Immigrant workers cleaning and caring in the shadows of affluence.* Berkeley: University of California Press.

Hunt, V., & Zajicek, A. (2008). Strategic intersectionality and the needs of disadvantaged populations: An intersectional analysis of organizational inclusion and participation. *Race, Gender & Class, 15*(3–4), 180–203.

King, D. (1988). Multiple jeopardy, multiple consciousness: The context of a Black feminist ideology. *Signs, 14*, 42–72.

Maramba, D. C. (2008). Understanding campus climate through the voice of Filipina/o American college students. *College Student Journal, 42*(4), 1045–1060.

McCall, L. (2005). The complexity of intersectionality. *Signs 30*(3), 1771–800.

McPhail, B. (2002). Gender-bias hate crime: A review. *Trauma, Violence and Abuse, 3*(2), 125–145.

Meyer, M. D. (2004). "We're too afraid of these imaginary tensions": Student organizing in lesbian, gay, bisexual and transgender campus communities. *Communication Studies, 55*(4), 499–514.

Perry, B. (2001). *In the name of hate: Understanding hate crimes.* New York, NY: Routledge.

Potter, S. J., Fountain, K., & Stapleton, J. G. (2012). Addressing sexual and relationship violence in the LGBT community using a bystander framework. *Harvard Review of Psychiatry, 20*(4), 201–208.

Rankin, S. R. (2005). Campus climates for sexual minorities. *New Directions for Student Services, 2005*(111), 17–23.

Rankin, S. R., & Reason, R. D. (2005). Differing perceptions: How students of color and White students perceive campus climate for underrepresented groups. *Journal of College Student Development, 46*(1), 43–61.

Reid, L. D., & Radhakrishnan, P. (2003). Race matters: The relation between race and general campus climate. *Cultural Diversity and Ethnic Minority Psychology, 9*(3), 263–275.

Ryan, M., Broad, K. L., Walsh, C. F., & Nutter, K. L. (2013). Professional allies: The storying of allies to LGBTQ students on a college campus. *Journal of Homosexuality, 60*(1), 83–104.

Solorzano, D., & Yosso, T. (2000). Critical race theory, racial microaggressions, and campus racial climate: The experiences of African American college students. *Journal of Negro Education, 69*(1–2), 60–73.

Stotzer, R. L., & Hossellman, E. (2012). Hate crimes on campus: Racial/ethnic diversity and campus safety. *Journal of Interpersonal Violence, 27*(4), 644–661.

Strolovitch, D. (2007) *Affirmative advocacy: Race, class and gender in interest group politics.* Chicago, IL: University of Chicago Press.

Umbach, P. D., & Kuh, G. D. (2006). Student experiences with diversity at liberal arts colleges: Another claim for distinctiveness. *Journal of Higher Education, 77*(1), 169–192.

8

BRINGING LIFE TO LEARNING

Civic Engagement, Intersections, and Transforming College Students

Amy Howard, Juliette Landphair, and Amanda Lineberry

Toward the end of high school, students around the nation rush to complete community service obligations to various institutions, including schools and churches. Indeed, more than one third of high school seniors volunteers on a regular basis (Child Trends Databank, 2014). Students often enter college eager to continue volunteer work in their new communities. Colleges and universities, meanwhile, increasingly recognize the educational potential of their surrounding towns and neighborhoods. The community's historical context and contemporary realities provide interactive settings for transformative learning. Rather than approach the community as a repository of campus philanthropy, these institutions bring students, faculty, and community partners together in efforts to understand and address community-identified needs.

Cross-institutional approaches to civic engagement, such as community-based learning (CBL) and full participation, which promotes the thriving of all people from multiple communities, provide powerful opportunities for college students' intellectual and personal development (Sturm, Eatman, Saltmarsh, & Bush, 2011). Undergirded by theoretical knowledge gained in the classroom, students involved in civic learning often start to recognize their own privileges and responsibilities as members of a community, nation, and world. They notice and question intersections in their own lives, including nationality, race, socioeconomic level, and status as a college student. Scholarly, activist, and leadership impulses may emerge for the first time and cause students to change their career trajectory and, more broadly, reformulate their concept of who they are: their core identity. As such, civic engagement often proves a pivotal, life-changing learning experience for college students.

Using full participation to frame, evaluate, and grow community engagement opportunities, colleges and universities can help students interpret their identities and others' identities as complex and intersectional. Within this framework, civic engagement helps students gain a deeper understanding of intersectional identities and their daily impact.

One Student's Experience With Civic Engagement

Amanda Lineberry vividly recalls how civic engagement changed her life. As a White, working-class student from Richmond, Virginia, Amanda grew up witnessing local activists' attempts to reconcile the city's identity as the capital of the Confederacy—memorialized along the grand Monument Avenue with imposing statues of Confederate leaders—with the equally important narratives of a thriving antebellum slave trade and robust twentieth-century civil rights movement. After Amanda enrolled at the University of Richmond and began working with the university's Bonner Center for Civic Engagement (CCE), however, she developed a passion for the region that transformed how she saw herself as a White female Richmonder and university student and how she saw her fellow Richmonders.

Amanda's Story

My interrogation of my privilege as a White person started in a high school English class. My teacher had assigned Richard Wright's (1940) *Native Son*, and I, a normally chatty student, found myself silent in classroom discussions about the book. Through the protagonist Bigger's story, I began to sense a systematic oppression of people of color that I could not name or describe, but for which I felt responsible. Each class, I would squirm in my plastic desk chair and stare down at the pages, hoping not to be called on. Looking back at my 17-year-old self, I see a girl wrestling with her first feelings of White guilt.

Nevertheless, the phrases "White guilt" and "White privilege" did not enter my vocabulary until I started college and began taking classes that confronted and questioned those concepts and traced their impact on American history and politics. I was one of a few local students at the University of Richmond, coming from a suburb less than a half hour away. I did not know much about the history of my own city other than that it was the former capital of the Confederacy. Through CBL courses, I began to unpack a more complex narrative. I discovered that Richmond was home to not only many Civil War battlefields, but also a thriving civil rights movement.

However, unlike the pristine parks that preserve the memories of the Civil War, the fight for racial equality in Richmond is difficult to spot today. Those social justice battlefields include neighborhoods that resisted and eventually surrendered to various urban renewal projects, such as the construction of Interstate 95 through the city's downtown—neighborhoods that were razed, smoothed over, and too often forgotten.

As a sophomore at the University of Richmond, I discovered one of these neighborhoods at a brown bag gathering hosted by the CCE. These lunches feature a community speaker or speakers who provide a public lecture followed by discussion. I met a community organizer, Jason Sawyer, who worked in a neighborhood that was new to me: Fulton, a predominantly Black, low- and middle-income neighborhood in Richmond's East End. The following summer, I was awarded a civic fellowship from the CCE that allowed me to intern with Jason at the Neighborhood Resource Center of Greater Fulton (NRC). Through that internship, I learned that Fulton was less than 12 miles from my suburban home. I learned that half of Fulton was destroyed in a 1970s urban renewal project after being categorized as a "slum." I learned that today, Fulton residents are working to reunite and strengthen that historic neighborhood and bolster a healthy community.

One of those residents was Rosa, who became a dear friend on a hot day in July. "Alright, your turn," Rosa said. "You go up there and knock on the next door." Rosa put a hand on her hip and breathed heavily. She had a number of health problems, including one that made it difficult for her to walk for long periods of time. Looking back, I appreciate more and more how difficult it must have been for Rosa to go door-to-door canvassing in July. And yet, there she was. And I, a 19-year-old White girl from a private liberal arts university, was tagging along with her.

Slightly nervous, I walked up about nine steps with a number of papers in my hand. A local nonprofit called Rebuilding Together was offering free home repairs for low-income seniors in Fulton. I was helping Rosa, a lifelong Fulton resident and chair of the Greater Fulton's Future Initiative's Housing Committee, go from house to house and hand out the applications for the repairs.

I took a quick breath and gave the door a hard, quick knock. Then I heard a sudden burst of sound behind me. I whipped around and looked at Rosa doubled over on the sidewalk at the bottom of the stairs, laughing hysterically.

"Rosa? What's so funny!?"

"Girl, you don't knock on doors like that in Fulton—especially a White girl like you! You sound like the cops!" She kept laughing and waved me down the steps. Better luck—with a softer knock—at the next house.

It was that day that Rosa took a liking to me and I to her. Every time she came into the NRC, I smiled and walked around my countertop workspace to give her a hug. She was a short, older, African American woman. She wore cornrows, hot pink lipstick, and almost always a smile. Later that summer, I drove her down to City Hall, where she accepted an award from the mayor for her work in Fulton. In my mind, she was a grassroots-organizing hero. I almost felt embarrassed to be myself around her—a White girl from the suburbs who was getting a stipend to do the work she had been doing every day for years. I came into my internship thinking I could be a valuable resource to a community in need. After working with Rosa, I felt like an incredibly privileged guest with a lot more to learn and receive than to give.

The reason that Rosa and I developed such a strong relationship is that we came to empathize with each other and move past our assumptions. Before that hot day in July, it was easy for Rosa and me to make assumptions about each other because of how different we were. I was a young White student at a private university on the other side of town. It would have been easy for Rosa to assume that I was very wealthy and perhaps indifferent to the systematic racism that tore down her childhood home. She was a single Black mother who was older than me, and I never thought we would have much in common. If we had never built a relationship, I would never have seen her as a friend, a compassionate mother, and an activist.

After that transformational summer turned into another fall semester, I kept looking for ways to express what I had learned in Fulton—the things that Rosa, the NRC, and the Greater Fulton's Future Initiative had taught me. Luckily, I was supported by faculty and staff members in the CCE and in the university's diversity and inclusion office, Common Ground, who helped me integrate my community-based experience into deeper opportunities for growth and learning. My civic fellowship mentor, Amy Howard, helped me reflect on my experience, develop ideas for a digital story about the Greater Fulton's Future Initiative, and write a reflection paper unpacking what I had learned that summer from experiences and readings. Cassie Price, manager of the Civic Fellows program, led discussions in which my peers and I reflected on our fellowships and deepened our learning through shared experiences, and she hosted a symposium with Howard in which we shared our learning with the broader campus community. Common Ground hosted a weekend-long, off-campus social justice leadership retreat that created an environment where students from diverse backgrounds bravely discussed concepts of privilege, oppression, identity, and empathy. They provided me with tools that helped me better understand myself and my experience in Fulton.

I followed that retreat with a political science class that helped me reconnect with Rosa. The professor, Jennifer Erkulwater, gave the class the option of writing a traditional academic paper or one that weaved in interviews with someone who had experienced the U.S. welfare system. I remembered Rosa talking about using welfare benefits as a single mother and as a person with severe health issues. I asked Rosa if she would be willing to share her experiences with me. Through talking to her, I realized how her experience with the welfare system had negatively affected her own sense of self-worth. At the same time, her work with the Greater Fulton's Future Initiative had greatly improved her sense of accomplishment and pride. She is a confident, award-winning, transformational community leader. The scholarship on welfare recipients could group her into a static identity ridden with stereotypes—a single Black mother on welfare. My civic engagement experience and research complicated that stereotype and helped me empathize with Rosa. She continues to inspire me, and her willingness to share her story with me helped me write the undergraduate paper of which I am most proud.

My fellowship with Rosa and the NRC also helped me understand the intersections of my own identity as a young White woman, a member of the working class, a University of Richmond student/alumna, and a Richmonder. Without that experience, my concept of community would not have expanded very far beyond my family and friends in my neighborhood. My sense of responsibility to Richmond would have been limited to the predominantly White suburban surroundings with which I was familiar. By pairing a civically engaged internship with an academic mentor, I made deep connections among what I learned about power, privilege, and identity on campus and the history and present reality of my hometown. After my fellowship, I took every class with "Richmond" in the title. I was hungry to learn how my education at the University of Richmond could better help me understand myself and my community and how I could fully participate in that community. I began to see my education as vital to my development as a citizen of Richmond.

Civic Engagement and Student Identity

Amanda's story supports research findings about the powerful effect of civic engagement on college student identity development. By working with diverse groups of people to understand and improve community concerns, students begin to appreciate perspectives beyond their own. Their empathy deepens, even at a developmental stage that is often self-focused. This growth counteracts challenges to empathy development among college students, such as increased communication online and by text (rather than face-to-face) and working and studying in a competitive culture that encourages selfishness over selflessness (Dolby, 2013). Students participating in civic learning witness how the exigencies of people's actual lives reflect knowledge gained in class about intractable social concerns. Their thinking grows more complicated, as does their sense of themselves as a participant in these social realities. This empathic learning prepares students for a critical outcome of a liberal education: understanding "the challenges of a diverse and unequal world" (AAC&U, 2015).

College students involved in civic learning often credit relationships with community members for shifting their views on the world and their roles in it. As one University of Richmond alumnus, Sean Hickey, recalled, mentoring students in an urban middle school "caused me to ask many questions of myself" (Hickey, 2014). Sean had developed close relationships with several mentees and had grown frustrated with the systems that had created his students' life circumstances, which were so different from his own. He began to wonder whether his mentoring made any difference in these systems or might even be unintentionally harmful. He concluded that approaching service as "inherently good" throws college students into "a state of mental security that facilitates neither improvement nor critical assessment of" that work. Sean's experience, while peculiar to him, exemplifies how college students engaged in the community often consider for the first time how their own presence and background figure into social and systemic hierarchies. As in Amanda's case, understanding social problems in context and reflecting on privilege and power afforded Sean the opportunity to examine his own identities and civic agency.

Through civic engagement, many students realize how their own identities give them advantages they had never before recognized. Previously unacknowledged identities often emerge in different community contexts. For instance, an African American student from a wealthy suburb might reformulate her identity as a person of color after working as the only non-White tutor in a program primarily serving low-income children of color. A middle-class student who had never known privation may observe poverty's effects on children, or a male student might witness the struggles of a single mother working in a low-wage job. Admitting one's privilege can be very difficult, especially for students who proclaim their tolerance by eschewing categorization (calling themselves color-blind, for instance). As social justice activist Paul Kivel observes, recognizing the benefits that come with Whiteness or any other privileged identity, including socioeconomic class or gender, may cause students guilt and embarrassment and even lead them to claim their own "legitimate victim status" in other identities, such as Jewish or female (Kivel, 2002). Yet, moving beyond those emotions proves rewarding as students gain a richer, more grounded knowledge of how community concerns evolve in the first place. They learn that their privileges and disadvantages can coexist, intersect, and impact the way they move through different environments.

Civic Engagement and Full Participation

Through approaches such as educationally grounded cocurricular programs and CBL, colleges provide laboratories for active democratic participation. For students, gaining classroom knowledge about public policies and different cultural contexts is often profound in itself. They begin to realize how little they knew or questioned in their own lives and value systems growing up, thereby reevaluating their own identities. Through institutional civic engagement programs, students such as Amanda and Sean meet people living within the systems they studied in the classroom. They work alongside faculty and citizens on issues affecting the community, such as food access or immigration and resettlement. The connection of theory with actual people and institutions provokes reflection that often reshapes students' sense of who they are and how they matter in the world.

In higher education, effective civic engagement requires committed institutional leaders, faculty, and staff. With that basic investment, a college can create three essential prongs of a civic engagement infrastructure: (a) the articulation of shared values to drive decisions and create coalitions, (b) the building and sustaining of partnerships on and off campus, (c) and the means to assess student learning as a result of civic engagement. Faculty, meanwhile, may seek to integrate CBL into their courses. With these building blocks, a campus can deepen and extend the impact of civic engagement for students, the campus, and the community.

At the University of Richmond, the CCE, founded in 2004, offers several modes of civic learning—applicable across institutional types—that strengthen the foundation of civic engagement work in higher education. For decades before the CCE was created, various offices and student organizations at the University of Richmond had engaged in CBL. The founding objective of the CCE was to combine those efforts and create new ones in an integrated, intentional, cross-campus approach to community engagement. The CCE's mission is to transform student learning, deepen faculty engagement, and partner with community organizations for social change by connecting the university and regional communities in collaborative and sustained partnerships. Courses, research projects, volunteerism, fellowships, discussion series, and reflections bring students, faculty, staff, and community partners together to explore educationally meaningful approaches to community-identified needs.

The CCE's work has been informed by its values and shaped by partnerships with faculty, staff, students, and community partners. Two values have proven particularly important: *full participation*—defined as an inclusive approach that seeks out and considers diverse perspectives, recognizes participants as whole people, and invites individuals to contribute meaningfully—and *collaboration*—defined as a process of cocreation that enhances the communities to which the university and its students belong. In *Full Participation: Building the Architecture for Diversity and Public Engagement in Higher Education*, Sturm and colleagues (2011) provided an aspirational framework for stronger collaborations between community engagement, access, and inclusion:

> Full participation is an affirmative value focused on creating institutions that enable people, whatever their identity, background, or institutional position, to thrive, realize their capabilities, engage meaningfully in institutional life, and contribute to the flourishing of others. (p. 5)

Using the full-participation lens to guide discussions and foster collaborations between diversity and community engagement offices opens possibilities for deeper campus-community partnerships and students' exploration of the complex intersections of their and others' identities.

At the CCE, the full-participation approach has prompted students, faculty, and staff to reconceptualize students' orientation to service. The full-participation mind-set raises important questions: How do we prepare and support students to think through issues of difference, privilege, and identity in our advising, orientation, and other touch points with students? How are the communities with which we are working represented in our orientations and literature? Are the *assets* in the community or site fully understood along with the challenges? How much historical and political context do we provide to situate social issues within larger structures? How do we encourage students to connect what they are learning in courses with their identities and their civic action? How can we work with other campus areas (e.g., diversity office, dean of students, religious life) to encourage students' reflection on their own lives and experiences through their civic engagement? By centering questions about who is and is not at the table in meetings and discussions, civic engagement professionals can further support meaningful reciprocity in campus-community partnerships. Full participation, then, opens up new ways of seeing and doing civic engagement with a focus on the "thriving" and meaningful engagement of all people—students, faculty, staff, community partners, and the clients they serve.

In seeking to strengthen civic engagement efforts, any campus can build upon existing partnerships with local community organizations and establish new ones. Creating and sustaining long-term partnerships based on trust, collaboration, and mutual respect are critical. Relationship building is the core of this work; when partners are valued as coeducators and knowledge creators, the collaboration deepens. Establishing trust between a campus staff or faculty member and a community organization representative, visiting sites, and encouraging honest dialogue about the partnership—including what is working and what is not—provide the necessary foundation for the dynamic and often messy work of CBL and civic engagement. Over the past decade, the CCE has established approximately 35 core partnerships. Through ongoing communication, these relationships have evolved as needed to support mutuality in student learning and meeting community-identified needs.

Assessment of student learning and development is integral to successful civic engagement efforts. In 2011, the CCE and the University of Richmond's Office for Institutional Effectiveness conducted focus groups with community partners and students who engage with CCE partner organizations. They wanted to know what students and the community partners who supervise and mentor them believed students were learning from their engagement experiences. The results, coupled with extensive reflection from CCE staff, resulted in the development of the following four aspirational learning outcomes for students engaged deeply and over time in various communities:

1. The CCE helps students understand the ways that difference, privilege, and power work in their own lives and in our society.
2. The CCE broadens and deepens students' thinking about complex and interconnected social issues affecting our world today.
3. The CCE prepares students for active citizenship.
4. The CCE prepares students for lives of active learning.

These learning outcomes have been incorporated into a dynamic cycle of assessment activities that measure specific student learning outcomes while also building a culture of generative and meaningful assessment among CCE staff and campus allies.

The CCE's Bonner Scholars program, a four-year student civic engagement program, provides an example of learning-based assessment. The CCE developed goal-focused prompts to guide Bonner Scholars' written reflections. As outlined in its first learning goal, for instance, the CCE helps students understand the ways that difference, privilege, and power work in their own lives and in our society. Through their experiences in CCE programs students will develop their

- understanding of their own identities and backgrounds;
- understanding of identities and backgrounds different from their own;

- understanding of the systemic forces that have shaped and continue to shape our different life experiences;
- attitudes of curiosity and openness about others; and
- capacity for empathy, learning to relate to and appreciate people different from themselves.

The CCE staff reviews selected write-ups and scores them on a rubric developed to understand how students learn through sustained community engagement. The resultant data inform the CCE's work, collaborations with other offices on campus, and efforts to realize the aspiration of full participation through the content, context, advising, educational programming, and reflection designed for students in CCE programs.

Qualitative assessment results demonstrate the ways in which educationally based civic engagement encourages identity contemplation at the intersections. In one reflection, a volunteer at a nonprofit working with ex-offenders reentering society noted, "The most satisfying aspect of my work . . . has been building relationships with program participants who have much different backgrounds than mine. It is so powerful to realize that no matter how different we are, it is possible to find common ground" (CCE, 2014, p. 25). A student working with patients and families from other countries seeking medical care in the United States explained, "I didn't realize how difficult it would be to try and connect with people who are so different from me. . . . [This experience has taught] me how to be more intentional and genuine in my interactions with people. I think it's okay that I don't completely understand things from their point of view, just that they may have a different one and I have to respect that" (CCE, 2014, p. 25). This experiential learning complicates and transforms how students see others—and themselves—in the world.

Inside the classroom, the connection between theory and practice afforded through CBL pedagogy can deepen students' learning. This high-impact practice—an active learning practice that, as research has shown, contributes to cumulative learning for students from many backgrounds—serves as another doorway for students to civically engage and reflect on their identities (Kuh, 2008). Amanda's research paper in her political science class is an excellent example of this. She was able to compare her experience in Fulton to current literature on social welfare and identity, challenging assumptions made about Rosa's identities. This, in turn, prompted her to reflect on her own identity. CBL courses can also serve as another site for universities to measure learning goals on identity and privilege, depending on the course and the mode of community engagement.

The CCE purposefully adopted a broad definition of *CBL* in seeking connections with faculty across the University of Richmond's five schools (business, leadership, arts and sciences, law, and professional and continuing studies). CBL modes include clinical education; study or service trips; service-learning; community partners in the classroom; organizational studies and consulting; teaching course materials in schools, prisons, and so on; producing creative works; and analysis and research for community partners. Faculty interested in designing a new CBL course or revising an existing course can apply to participate in a faculty fellows program and a yearlong faculty learning community.

Connecting with faculty from other departments and schools and meeting community partners together with CCE staff catalyze new relationships and collaborations across campus and in the community. A broad definition of *CBL* with which many faculty can identify and consultation with faculty members on course design, learning outcomes, and community partnership have contributed to the increase in CBL courses from approximately 48 in 2008–2009 to 87 across five schools in 2013–2014. Through these courses, both faculty and students deepen their engagement in local and global communities and learning.

The CCE is among several campus offices that aim to support students' understanding of themselves and the world around them. Recognizing that students view themselves as a whole made up of various parts, the CCE collaborates with other offices in bolstering a holistic approach to the college experience. Students in CCE programs, for example, are recommended for the Office of Common Ground's EnVision social justice retreat, where participants "explore systemic and institutional issues of power and privilege and learn how to apply their knowledge to become effective change agents." This relationship encouraged Amanda to attend EnVision, where she further unpacked her identity and her understanding of identity as complex and intersectional. Likewise, the Office of Common Ground, the Office of Living and Learning, the Women Involved in Living and Learning (WILL) program, the Office of Multicultural Affairs, the chaplaincy, and the dean of students offices work together to support and advise students in their academic and cocurricular explorations. This type of collaboration requires no new resources; it does require, however, a shared vision of holistic student learning and development.

Conclusion

For most students, college is a time of profound personal and intellectual change. Leaving home, gaining new knowledge, meeting people on and off campus, and joining organizations combine to throw long-held values into question. During their college years, many students realize their own capacity to discern who they are and who they want to become. This process does not occur in one class or one club; it occurs across time and across places where learning and discussion are encouraged. It can be both exciting and dispiriting. By literally and intellectually bringing college students into the realities of other people's lives thoughtfully and respectfully, civic engagement has the power to transform students' understanding of the intersections of their identities in deep and lasting ways. And as the United States continues to diversify and connect with nations across the world, the empathic and cognitive skills that students gain through civic engagement become all the more important.

References

Association of American Colleges and Universities (AAC&U). (2015). Global learning. Retrieved from https://www.aacu.org/resources/global-learning

Bonner Center for Civic Engagement (CCE). (2014). *Annual impact report: 2013–2014*. Richmond, VA: Bonner Center for Civic Engagement.

Child Trends Databank. (2014). *Volunteering*. Retrieved from http://www.childtrends.org/?indicators=volunteering

Dolby, N. (2013). The decline of empathy and the future of liberal education. Retrieved from https://www.aacu.org/liberaleducation/2013/spring/dolby

Hickey, S. (2014, October 14). Deconstructing service: Bonner scholar reflects on his four years of community service. Retrieved from http://news.richmond.edu/features/kp4/article/-/12244/deconstructing-service-bonner-scholar-reflects-on-his-four-years-of-community-service-.html

Kivel, P. (2002). *Uprooting racism: How White people can work for social justice*. Gabriola Island, Canada: New Society.

Konrath, S. H., O'Brien, E. H., & Hsing, C. (2011). Changes in dispositional empathy in American college students over time: A meta-analysis. *Personality and Social Psychology Review, 15*(2), 180–198.

Kuh, G. D. (2008). High-impact practices: What they are, who has access to them, and why they matter. Retrieved from http://secure.aacu.org/store/detail.aspx?id=E-HIGHIMP

Sturm, S., Eatman, T., Saltmarsh, J., & Bush, A. (2011, September). Full participation: Building the architecture for diversity and public engagement in higher education. Retrieved from http://imaginingamerica.org/research/full-participation/history/

PART THREE

LEARNING

DIVERSIFYING DIVERSITY, DIVERSIFYING DISABILITY

Danielle R. Picard and Nancy L. Chick

*I have come to understand that much of what I took as neutral teaching practice actually
functions to keep our courses less accessible to students from non-traditional backgrounds. . . .
(Almost) all traditionally taught courses are unintentionally but nevertheless deeply biased in ways
that make substantial differences in performance for many students.*
—Nelson, 1996, p. 165

Most of the scholarship on teaching, learning, and diversity focuses on race, or perhaps gender, culture, or nationality. In a meta-analysis, Bowman (2010) explained this more specific focus of the research: "For many college students," he observed, "race is the defining or most salient dimension of diversity" (p. 21). In addition, the benefits of racial diversity are not limited to the more widely cited changes in students' attitudes and values. They extend to improvement in cognitive development, critical thinking, and problem-solving skills because they are likely to "trigger disequilibrium and effortful thinking" (p. 21). At the same time, Bowman warned that the known impact of racial diversity should not "overshadow the benefits associated with all diversity interactions" (p. 21). Curşeu and Pluut (2013), for example, demonstrated that groupwork involving students of varied genders, nations, and motivations for understanding leads to more complex thinking. Their study reminds us that identities are not singular; they are in fact *intersectional*, or formed and informed by the interlocking phenomena of race, class, gender, sexuality, and other identity categories (Crenshaw, 1991).

Unfortunately, rarely are students with dyslexia, visual impairments, or multiple sclerosis, to name a few disabilities, integrated into these discussions of increasing the diversity of the college classroom.[1] An intersectional perspective, such as that offered in this book, brings in considerations of ability and disability, wedging open conversations about diversity and inclusive classrooms. Indeed, recognizing the interconnectedness of identity traits and sources of oppression shows us that the theorizing about racial diversity can help us understand and respond to broader notions of diversity and difference. Perhaps paradoxically, when we broaden our understanding of diversity by identifying multiple identity characteristics to ensure deliberate actions toward understanding and inclusion, our list is rarely comprehensive; it inevitably omits someone, becomes inadvertently exclusive, and thus "make[s] substantial differences in performance for many students" (Nelson, 1996, p. 165). Thus, we encourage reading this chapter not in isolation but in context with the other chapters in this book as we all explore how diversity improves experiences for all students. Our assets-based approach reaches beyond the deficit model of focusing solely on accommodations and highlights the universal benefits of including disability in our efforts to create inclusive classrooms.

The Implications of Language

The first challenge of addressing disability in the classroom is language. While the terms *race, gender,* and *nationality* are arguably unbiased words by themselves, the term *disability* is not. Its prefix connotes deficiency and abnormality, a label that perpetuates false stereotypes in which students who are deaf or use a wheelchair, for instance, are not as capable as their peers.

Beyond the term itself is the language used for the human beings in the classroom. "A disabled student" expresses a singular identity, while the subtle shift to "a student who has a disability" makes room for an intersectional or multilayered identity and prioritizes the student over the disability, an ethos that also reminds us to refer to the disability only when it is relevant to the situation.[2] For instance, when praising exam grades, it is often irrelevant and inappropriate to mention that the highest score was earned by a student with dyslexia.

As with most labels, the generic term *disability* conflates an array of situations, glossing over the particularities of a student's circumstances. The abilities of one student under this umbrella term may be very unlike another—a point that requires us to pause and consider the implications of acknowledging difference. McLaren (1995) identified four assumptions about racial differences that extrapolate effectively to any discussion of difference:

1. People who are different are "add-ons" who lack something necessary and should be assimilated into the mainstream to make up for the deficit (p. 37).
2. People who are different are *not different* but in fact the same: Everyone is a human being. Focusing on differences is inappropriate. (This generic "human being" is actually a dominant norm erasing important elements of the identities of "others.")
3. People who are different are *uniquely different*, in singular, simple, and essential ways, and we must focus solely on those differences.
4. People who are different are different for a variety of complex social reasons, leading to important differences "*between* and *among* groups" that we must acknowledge (p. 43).

The last perspective, which McLaren called "critical" (in the sense of critical thinking, not skeptical) honors the complexity of causes, identities, and needs of groups. It embraces a "both/and" view in which groups are similar in important ways and different in important ways, neither of which should be ignored. Because of the similarities, McLaren's notions of difference apply to a variety of human contexts. Because of the differences, the complexities of "disability" matter, so we continue interrogating "neutral teaching practice."

Disabilities vary in terms of duration (temporary, relapsing, or long-term), type (cognitive, physical, psychological, visual, auditory), and visibility (visible or hidden). It is useful to think of examples, identifying specific situations and solutions. A student with a broken arm, for instance, may be unable to take traditional notes, so an instructor may ask a classmate to share notes for a few weeks. Students with chronic health disorders (e.g., epilepsy, Crohn's disease, diabetes, migraine headaches) may need an occasional grace period in submitting work, leniency on class participation and attendance policies, or the freedom to get up and leave the classroom without calling attention to what some might consider a disruption. Students with long-term physical impairments, such as hearing loss, low vision, and mobility difficulties, may require instructors to rethink methods of instruction and types of student engagement. Students with post-traumatic stress disorder (PTSD), anxiety and mood disorders, or Asperger's syndrome may be uncomfortable in some group situations and need alternative ways to contribute or the ability to quietly step outside the classroom if a conversation or situation becomes overwhelming. Students with traumatic brain injuries or learning disabilities may need variation in class format to prevent fatigue from focusing on a single mode of instruction. All of these practices, however, would benefit all students without disrupting the essential learning goals of a course.

Disabilities can also be inconspicuous. A student with a chronic pain dis-order or a relapsing condition, like multiple sclerosis, may look and act like the other students, unless she chooses (or is forced) to disclose her situation. This invisibility causes others to assume that, because she "looks fine," there is no problem in introducing physical activities, such as rearranging desks or moving around the room.

Designing for Inclusion

As with all effective teaching, purposeful actions create inclusive classrooms. Even with the best of intentions, instructors cannot simply implement this fix or follow that template but instead must begin with purposeful reflection and awareness of their specific students.

One common misconception about teaching students with disabilities is that accommodations will dilute or distract from the nature of a course. Instructors may hesitate out of loyalty to course content and the discipline's signature pedagogies, both of which are important to authentic learning. However, revisiting a course through the lens of Wiggins and McTighe's (2006) classic "backward design" (p. 15) approach will reveal that a class can accommodate students with different needs without sacrificing its essential core. In this course (re)design process, instructors first name what they want students to learn—not just skills and concepts, but overarching or "enduring understandings" (pp. 128–130)—then identify assessments that will make visible students' progress in these learning goals, and finally design activities to encourage plenty of practice. This process builds the details of the course, including ways to accommodate the specific needs of students, only after identifying the foundation that will undergird these details.

Similarly, in her response to the skeptical "how much is enough?" con-cerns about accommodations, Scott (1997) encouraged instructors to ask the following questions: What is the purpose of the course? What methods of instruction are absolutely necessary, and why? What outcomes are abso-lutely required of all students, and why? What methods of assessing student outcomes are absolutely necessary, and why? What are acceptable levels of performance on these student outcome measures? Consider, for example, the following scenario:

> *During a common creativity activity, Dr. Grant asked her business students to walk around the room and share an elaborate gesticulation when they made eye contact with a peer. A student asked if there was another way for students to participate if they did not feel comfortable with these plans. Dr. Grant said*

yes, but most students should have fun with it if they are able to do so. As the exercise went on, noticing a few students simply walking to a classmate and standing still, she reminded them of the importance of the gesticulations for the activity. She then turned and made eye contact with Jessie, who turned bright red and nervously whispered, "I just had a lumpectomy, and I can't really move around right now." Jessie had not planned to tell anyone about her surgery.

In this anecdote, Grant's goal of encouraging creative thinking by performing something unfamiliar is achievable through a range of options, such as making elaborate gestures, inventing a new word, or developing a new use for a familiar object like a paperclip. Similarly, participation in lab settings—critical for many natural science classes—may occur in a variety of forms (e.g., observation, listening, handling equipment, collecting data). Also, offering alternative exam formats, such as an in-class written essay exam, an out-of-class timed writing with voice recognition software, or an in-person oral exam, may accomplish the same essential learning goals while also giving an equal chance to students who have limited use of their hands or other difficulties within the traditional exam format (Bourke, Strehorn, & Silver, 2000; Scott, 1997).

Another misconception about creating such inclusive classrooms is that the other students' experiences will be disrupted. The notion of inclusive design challenges this thinking by acknowledging that all students have differing needs, and many of the barriers and biases that we assume affect a few students in fact affect all students. Like McLaren's taxonomy, this principle demands that we acknowledge the differences among students, creating classrooms that acknowledge a range of diversities while also respecting individual identities.

While inclusive design is based on the principles of universal design, we recognize that aspects of sex, gender, intersectionality, age, race, ability, and size are too diverse to be "universally" accommodated, which often means that some factors are prioritized at the expense of others (Hamraie, 2013). Instead, inclusive design encourages instructors to develop course materials, content, and instruction to benefit the specific learners in their specific classrooms. It emphasizes "giving students what they need to accrue the same outcomes as others in a particular context" (Harper, 2009, p. 42) and is thus undergirded by a commitment to equity in the classroom, rather than assuming a blind or generic universalism that treats all students as the same. Here, we offer some recommendations that are applicable across the curriculum, that will not alter key disciplinary content or pedagogies, and that illustrate an approach to creating effective classrooms for a greater number of students.

Know Your Students

Good teaching practice includes learning students' names and perhaps a few other details relevant to the course. Extending this practice to invite safe disclosure is an important first step. A brief questionnaire on the first day of class may end with "Is there anything you would like me to know about you?" or "Are there any circumstances that would make our learning environment and activities difficult for you?" This encourages students like Jessie in the earlier anecdote to privately share important challenges that may not meet accommodations requirements or that may be uncomfortable for the student to discuss in person.

Reflect on the Effects of Stigma

Students with disabilities—visible or invisible—face negative stereotypes held by others and even themselves. While we may focus on the attitudes of the other students, Davis (2009) pointed to the importance of the instructor's beliefs and biases in creating an inclusive environment:

> Your attitudes and values not only influence the attitudes and values of your students, but they can affect the way you teach, particularly your assumptions about students, . . . which can lead to unequal learning outcomes for those in your classes. (p. 58)

Some stigmas, especially those connected to skills relevant in class, may cause students to resist telling the instructor. Students with learning disabilities, for example, may be perceived as less intelligent (May & Stone, 2010), when in reality they simply receive, process, store, and/or respond to information differently (National Center for Learning Disabilities, 2014). Students who use a wheelchair are frequently thought to also have a mental disability (Scorgie, Kildal, & Wilgosh, 2010), and students like Jessie from the previous anecdote may worry that classmates will see only their cancer or feel forced to defend a "hidden" condition.

Respect Students' Privacy

As with other personal information (some protected by the Family Educational Rights and Privacy Act, some not), instructors should always assume confidentiality and respect the privacy of all students. A student's disclosure of a disability is always voluntary. The creativity exercise in the previous anecdote forces Jessie's hand, and even though she whispers, her classmates will realize that something is wrong, and some may even overhear.

Recognize the Role of Identity in the Classroom

A traditional approach to teaching students with disabilities is based on the assumption that they must be "assisted" to do the "normal" work of the course, which positions the student as an instructor's problem. Assuming instead that all students bring specific identities and assets to the learning environment changes the relationship between instructor and student. University students are often coming to terms with their identities, and students with disabilities contend with the abled-disabled dichotomy in their identity formation (Myers, 2015). Jessie, for instance, does not want her identity to be reduced to her diagnosis. "Ability allies" (Myers, 2015, p. 143) promote individualized and thoughtful interactions with and between students and facilitate respectful classroom spaces where students can (but do not have to) self-disclose and where they can grapple with the ways their identities are similar to and different from their peers'. Such allies also nurture conversations about how students' identities play into the university setting and beyond.

Be Proactive

The university may be the first instance in which students with disabilities have to advocate for themselves, as they are responsible for requesting accommodations through the appropriate office and then notifying instructors, actions often required at the very beginning of a course. The process requires students to negotiate what may feel like the "burden" of access and inclusion. Harper (2009), in his discussion of developing "race-consciousness," encouraged instructors to become "educationally purposeful" (p. 38), "equity-minded" (p. 43), and intentionally and proactively inclusive by acknowledging the differing situations and needs of the students in the classroom. Instructors' and institutional attitudes of "only determining *what students do* to become engaged" are then replaced by planning "*what educators do* to engage students" (p. 41). This action can begin before classes even start. Effective syllabi will not only communicate important policies and information (e.g., identify the institution's resources for tutoring services, mental health support, and disability resources) but also establish the personality and ethics of the classroom. Instructors can give students as much preparatory information as possible by making the schedule, texts, due dates for assignments, and other key materials available before registration. Course syllabi can also include a statement explicitly establishing the classroom as a welcoming environment for all students, such as the following:

> This class respects and welcomes students of all backgrounds, identities, and abilities. If there are circumstances that make our learning environ-

ment and activities difficult, if you have medical information that you need to share with me, or if you need specific arrangements in case the building needs to be evacuated, please let me know. I am committed to creating an effective learning environment for all students, but I can only do so if you discuss your needs with me as early as possible. I promise to maintain the confidentiality of these discussions. If appropriate, also contact the Disability Services Office to get more information about specific accommodations.

These invitations should not, however, be limited to the beginning of the course. If Jessie's surgery came unexpectedly in the third week of the semester, she would not have shared it with her professor earlier. Consistently offering a range of choices and regularly prefacing activities with "as you are able" will proactively include students throughout the semester.

Use Multiple Modes of Communication

As disciplinary content becomes increasingly difficult, efforts to make it accessible benefit all students' learning. Part of good teaching involves helping novices become familiar with unfamiliar and challenging concepts and language. Nelson (1996) provided lecture outlines and key questions, a practice that not only helps students with interpreters but also lets his students focus on learning the ideas rather than focusing on the kinds of note taking or studying that take a lot of work "without accomplishing much" (p. 178). Expanding the foregoing creativity exercise to include not only movement but also spoken language, design thinking, and drawing is more inclusive, but it also demonstrates multiple instances of creative thinking. Videos shown in class can more effectively support the learning of all students by using closed-captioning, providing transcripts, describing on-screen action, allowing students to check out the video on their own, and outlining the role the video plays in the day's lesson. These choices allow all students to engage with the material in multiple ways, as well as reduce the access barrier for students who cannot hear the audio or see nonverbalized actions and those with disorders like photosensitive epilepsy who may experience seizures with flashing lights or images (Burgstahler & Cory, 2010; Silver, Bourke, & Strehorn, 1998).

Revisit the Goals of Assessment

Nelson (1996) described unfair and irrelevant biases embedded in rigid notions of deadlines and "one-shot grading," practices that ground assessment and grades in "social class behaviors, such as the ability to complete assignments on time, rather than on the ability to understand and apply the content" (p. 169). The result is that these traditions may reinforce class—and other—barriers by penalizing students for what we perceive as an unwilling-ness or inability "to do what it [takes] to obtain a professional job." More precise alignment of assessment to measure essential learning outcomes improves the learning of all students without sacrificing rigor. For example, if mastery of material is the goal, rather than simply getting it right the first time, quizzes can be redesigned to allow multiple attempts without penalty (Nevid & Mahon, 2009). Online environments are ideal for this kind of assessment, though colors, fonts, and formats should be scrutinized for stu-dents with low vision or color blindness.[3] Additionally, reminders of which course materials provide relevant information reinforce conceptual thinking rather than memorization.

Similarly, many instructors require class participation, but talking in a large group (like using wild gestures to demonstrate creative thinking) may not be the only way students can practice their understanding. Time to com-pose thoughts through writing will support greater reflection in all students and help some feel more prepared to speak in a large group. Small-group dis-cussions can more effectively engage introverted students, content novices, and students with PTSD.

Consider Space and Location

Instructors often inspect classroom spaces to accommodate their typical activities, such as lecturing with media, using small groups, ensuring access to outlets for laptop use, or blocking out seating in the back to keep students in the front of the hall. This is also an ideal time to consider access. For exam-ple, planning movement activities to fit the classroom space should include plans for students like Jessie who struggle with movement. Also, large, tiered lecture halls are not only challenging for most active learning techniques, but also unwelcoming to students who use canes or are hard of hearing, and projection screens may be too distant for students with low vision.

Additionally, office hours can rotate between the instructor's office and a more accessible or neutral meeting area, such as the library or student center. Such flexibility demonstrates a more thoughtful invitation for students who feel intimidated coming to what they perceive as an instructor's "private space" or who struggle to navigate an office's tight spaces.

Conclusion

Designing courses in ways that acknowledge students' intersectional iden-tities, including those related to disability, opens up the classroom to all students by valuing their experiences and supporting their learning with intentionality and effective teaching practices. This process begins with questioning seemingly "neutral" beliefs about approaches to teaching and learning. Then, by incorporating our recommendations during the planning and running of a course, educators can engage with the complexity of diversity as they strive to create truly inclusive classrooms.

Notes

1. This chapter originated in a teaching guide written by Picard for the Vanderbilt University Center for Teaching.

2. For more information on terminology, see the guide provided by the National Center on Disability and Journalism: ncdj.org/style-guide/

3. For more on creating color-blind-accessible figures and presentations, see M. Okabe and K. Ito, "Color Universal Design (CUD): How to Make Figures and Presentations That Are Friendly to Colorblind People." J*Fly Data Depository.

References

Bourke, A. B., Strehorn, K. C., & Silver, P. (2000). Faculty members' provision of instructional accommodations to students with LD. *Journal of Learning Disabilities, 33*(1), 26–32.

Bowman, N. A. (2010). College diversity experiences and cognitive development: A meta-analysis. *Review of Educational Research, 80*(1), 4–33. doi:10.3102/0034654309352495

Burgstahler, S., & Cory, R. (2010). *Universal design in higher education: From principles to practice.* Cambridge, MA: Harvard Education Press.

Cortiella, C., & Horowitz, S. H. (2014). *The state of learning disabilities: Facts, trends and emerging issues.* (3rd ed.). New York, NY: National Center for Learning Disabilities.

Crenshaw, K. (1991, July). Mapping the margins: Intersectionality, identity politics, and violence against women of color. *Stanford Law Review, 43*(6), 1241–1299.

Curşeu, P. L., & Pluut, H. (2013). Student groups as learning entities: The effect of group diversity and teamwork quality on groups' cognitive complexity. *Studies in Higher Education, 38*(1), 87–103.

Davis, B. G. (2009). *Tools for teaching.* San Francisco, CA: Jossey-Bass.

Hamraie, A. (2013). Designing collective access: A feminist disability theory of universal design. *Disability Studies Quarterly, 33*(4). Retrieved from http://dsq-sds.org/article/view/3871/3411

Harper, S. R. (2009). Race-conscious student engagement practices and the equitable distribution of enriching educational experiences. *Liberal Education, 95*(4), 38–45.

May, A. L., & Stone, C. A. (2010). Stereotypes of individuals with learning disabilities: Views of college students with and without learning disabilities. *Journal of Learning Disabilities, 43*(6), 483–499. doi:10.1177/0022219409355483

McLaren, P. (1995). White terror and oppositional agency: Towards a critical multiculturalism. In C. E. Sleeter & P. McLaren (Eds.), *Multicultural education, critical pedagogy, and the politics of difference* (pp. 33–70) Albany: State University of New York Press.

Myers, K. A. (2015). Students with disabilities: From success to significance. In P. A. Sasso & J. L. DeVitis (Eds.), *Today's college students: A reader* (pp. 141–150). New York, NY: Peter Lang.

Nelson, C. E. (1996). Student diversity requires different approaches to college teaching, even in math and science. *American Behavioral Scientist, 40*(2), 165–175.

Nelson, C. E. (1999). On the persistence of unicorns: The trade-off between content and critical thinking. In B. A. Pescosolido & R. Aminzade (Eds.), *The social worlds of higher education: Handbook for teaching in a new century* (pp. 168–185). Thousand Oaks, CA: Pine Forge Press.

Nevid, J. S., & Mahon, K. (2009). Mastery quizzing as a signaling device to cue attention to lecture material. *Teaching of Psychology, 36,* 29–32. doi:10.1080/0098 6280802529152

Scorgie, K., Kildal, L., & Wilgosh, L. (2010). Post-secondary students with disabilities: Issues related to empowerment and self-determination. *Developmental Disabilities Bulletin, 38*(1–2), 133–145.

Scott, S. S. (1997). Accommodating college students with learning disabilities: How much is enough? *Innovative Higher Education, 22*(2), 85–99.

Silver, P., Bourke, A., & Strehorn, K. C. (1998). Universal instructional design in higher education: An approach for inclusion. *Equity & Excellence in Education, 31*(2), 47–51.

Wiggins, G. P., & McTighe, J. (2006). *Understanding by design.* Upper Saddle River, NJ: Pearson Education.

10

LEADERSHIP FOR A GLOBAL, CARING SOCIETY

Ed Taylor

This chapter offers a glimpse into an undergraduate seminar on leadership and morality with undergraduates primarily from the United States and students on an exchange from Japan. It serves as a case study of the intersections between the diverse identities and experiences that students brought to the classroom, as well as those they discovered as they moved through the quarter and in conversations with each other. Although the course took place in a single classroom at a large public university, it is relevant to teaching, learning, and student engagement in any college or university setting that seeks to help students explore and share meaning and identity.

Thinking of these students—many far from home for the first time, some experiencing the classroom as ethnic minorities for the first time—led me to develop a course anchored in my own experience as a first-generation African American college student from Southern California who chose to attend a predominantly White private university in Spokane, Washington. My own transition to Spokane was not quite the same as traveling to another country, but the domestic experience had many similarities with a foreign one. I at least had the advantage of speaking the same language as my peers, but that experience taught me the challenges that may come with leaving home for the first time and arriving at a new campus that feels like a strange land.

This chapter describes the course that my students and I created together. I may have designed the class, but I had no idea how the full and open engagement of students from two very different cultures would end up shaping it. Although not deliberately focused on intersectionality, my course led students to think and talk about the intersectionalities in the lives of Japanese

I would like to thank my colleague Catharine Beyer for her thoughtful guidance, partnership, and for always editing.

and American leaders, as well as to discover and acknowledge those intersectionalities in their own lives.

The Course Design

In planning the course, I tried to imagine a seminar that would bring to bear what I know about student development, student success, and student engagement. Students in research universities do better when they are active in their learning, are engaged in learning communities, are sufficiently challenged, have opportunities to research and share common intellectual experiences, and explore questions that matter to them and the world they will inhabit (Beyer, Gillmore, & Fisher, 2007; Kuh, 2008). With that in mind, along with the memory of my own experience, I designed the United States–Japan leadership seminar. I hoped to develop an understanding of leadership and friendship, as well as a sense of community, among the next generation of leaders in each country with an emphasis on creating space for students' "social identities" to emerge (Rydell, McConnell, & Beilock, 2009) through classroom discourse and formation of a learning community. The course was also intended to bring together students who represented the relationship between two of the world's most powerful democracies and economies in a way that would transcend boundaries and require consideration of global issues and an understanding of the self and others.

I hoped to foster dialogue among future leaders across areas of study to discuss leadership, morality, citizenship, and historical and current issues in bilateral relations, as well as issues reaching beyond our two countries. I hoped the students would engage each other in conversation about shared cultural experiences with the overall goal of taking steps toward the formation of leaders who might foster a more caring global community—*Omoiyari no aru kokusai shakai ni mukete no ridashippu* [leadership toward a caring community]—and, on an individual basis, nurture the beginnings of lifelong friendships.

Finally, I wanted to create a class where the students' lives and what they were experiencing together as they entered the new culture that is college would be a big part of the "content." In a sense, their experience and what they brought to it would be an essential and explicit part of the course's design.

I gave students two guidelines for the course. First, I told them that the course would function as a seminar. I would offer some initial questions and thoughts, but the course would depend largely on each student participating in class discussion. I would expect thoughtful commentary and critical thinking about global leadership and about who we are and who we intend to be in the world.

Second, I emphasized that my aim was for us to engage in a "moral conversation." The Latin root of the word "conversation" is *conversari*. It means to live with, to keep company with, to turn around, to oppose. Thus, for me, a dialogue and conversation is literally a manner of living whereby people keep company with each other and talk together in good faith in order to exchange ideas—sometimes in agreement, sometimes in opposition. Bakhtin's writings on the dialogic nature of texts provide the basis for learning—the process of multiple voices coming into contact, within and across speaker-produced statements (Ballenger, 1997).

I let students know that I hoped our conversation would transcend some of the traditional confines of disciplinary boundaries and the fragmentation of knowledge that accompanies those boundaries to make collective meaning (Bakhtin, 1981). I said that I wanted us to pose questions that require interdisciplinary answers, broad conceptualizations, and thoughtful interpretations.

Furthermore, this conversation would be "moral," from the Latin *moralis* (custom). A moral conversation is one that emphasizes the fundamental worth and dignity of each person who participates in the exchange.

The Course Experience

Autumn quarter in Seattle on the campus of the University of Washington (UW) is a sight to behold. The campus is bustling with students, the sun is shining, and the campus landscape is marvelous. Thinking about the arc of the Seattle autumn, I told the students that while the main concept of the course would remain constant, our week-to-week schedule would change—mostly depending on the weather. My plan was to get us outside as much as possible, enjoying the beauty and also stepping intentionally out of our traditional classroom to explore the course's intersecting themes.

Session I

I began by asking the students to offer a brief introduction to themselves in whatever language they chose. I informed them that in class today they themselves were the "text," and we would listen carefully to and read each other. I was not surprised to observe the degree to which the students from Japan spoke English and Japanese and understood the English of their peers, nor was I surprised by how wary and cautious the students were with one another. All the students described their majors, where they were from, and what they hoped to learn—standard introductions before the customary walk through the syllabus. One surprise to me was that although most of the students in the course were incoming freshmen from Japan and the United States, students' backgrounds included Vietnam and the Netherlands, and a few students were upperclassmen.

I decided to end the first session on a single note—curiosity. I asked them to enter into our next conversation curious about each other and the fact that we would be here together for 10 weeks.

Session II

I prompted the students to go around the room again and answer a specific question: "What significant learning occurred for you this week?"

Yuko,[1] a freshman from Japan who plans to study religion and international affairs at her home institution in Japan, began the discussion with her response. "I can't think of anything significant that I've learned this week," she said.

I asked Yuko to consider the question another way. "Will you tell us about your first week as a student in the United States?"

Yuko answered, "Well, I'm pretty excited and don't really know anyone, but the place is so alive. But I'm a little nervous and I have a question for you. In Japan, we don't really talk that much in class. Is it expected that we will be asked to speak in our classes here at UW? I was told that we might have to express our opinions. Is that true?"

I asked the class to consider Yuko's question. Derek, a UW junior from Seattle who enrolled in the class because he found the course title interesting, replied, "Yeah, you'll be asked to speak sometimes but you don't always have to know all of the answers. It's okay to say 'I don't know the answer.'"

As I continued around the circle with the question of weekly learning, Lani thought for a moment and replied, "I woke up this morning trying to make sense of what I think about when I am awake and even when I sleep. My mind is always working, but I am not sure it is working on the right things. There is just so much to learn and so much to take in right now. I really need to figure out what to study and decide where I am going to go after college is over for me."

Lani came to UW from a Seattle suburb and was in his first quarter at the university. Although he finished the last two years of high school in Seattle, he spent his formative years in Vietnam and very much identified with the culture and people of Vietnam. He expressed interest in returning to his homeland to serve or perhaps teach.

For Mona, a senior who enrolled in the class because it "seemed interesting," the subject of sleep and dreaming touched a nerve. She said, "I am applying to medical school and I take the MCAT soon. Talk about losing sleep. What if I do horribly? I want to do well, but I guess the bigger question is whether I want to be a doctor."

Melissa, a student on an exchange from the Netherlands, followed the line of thinking about dreams. She replied, "You know I had my first dream in English? I am from the Netherlands, and I've never had a dream in another language before. That was really interesting."

After completing the round of reflections on their learning during the week, I asked the students to close their notebooks and follow me outside to the university's central plaza in front of Suzzallo Library, the most recognizable building on campus. In niches atop the building are 18 terra-cotta figures of influential thinkers selected by faculty. These include Moses, Louis Pasteur, Shakespeare, Galileo, Plato, Benjamin Franklin, Herodotus, Darwin, Homer, Grotius, and more.

We stood in the Seattle sunlight, looking up at the figures. I asked the students to consider this the text for the day. Who are these people and why do you think the faculty chose them? What do they represent? Who is missing? All of the students had walked in front of the library before, and some had noticed the figures but had not stopped to identify who they were or think about how they were chosen and why. We discussed the importance of simple observations of where we are each day—of our unique intersections with the physical world around us.

Session III

The following week we had established a routine. I would bring cookies, and the students would begin their "round" in response to a question. Hiro, who plans to study Japanese law in Japan, began the discussion. He said, "I've been thinking about the question you are going to ask and I thought of something if you don't mind. . . . I went to church for the first time in my life. I was asked by some friends to come with them on Sunday. So that was a first for me."

Hiro thanked the class for listening and then prompted the next student to speak. But I interrupted, saying, "Before we go on, does anyone have a question for Hiro?"

Lani asked, "Well, what was it like?"

Hiro responded, "It was so interesting. I thought mostly about what my parents would think about me being there because I wasn't really raised to believe in God. But I do wonder."

Yuko asked, "What do you believe? I do have to say, I don't really believe in God but I think of myself as being very spiritual. Do you plan to go again?"

Hiro said, "I think I will. It was kind of interesting to think about what people believe and why."

I told the students that in the following weeks, our text would not be buildings and icons but documents, beginning with parts of the U.S. Bill of Rights and of the Constitution of Japan. I handed each of them copies and asked them to be prepared to read parts aloud and to pay particular attention to language, intent, structure, and context.

Session IV

By the time I entered our small seminar room, everyone was there. We began right away with one of many examples to come of assumptions about the social contexts of our campuses.

Andrew spoke first. "This was a busy weekend because I play in the marching band, and we played for hours and hours. We had a pregame event on Friday and played most of the day on Saturday."

Yuko said, "I don't understand. Why are you playing for so many hours?"

Andrew answered, "I forgot to mention that in this country we have big football stadiums and thousands of people come to see this sport. I play in the band and we kind of get people excited and play through the game. You'll have to come to one before you go back to Japan."

Following the round of what their weeks had brought them, we read the U.S. Bill of Rights aloud, each student taking a part, followed by the Japanese Constitution. The students read the main portions of both documents carefully and deliberately. They compared the intent of the two documents and discussed freedom of religion, protection from unreasonable searches and seizures, and due process. We took care to discuss the Japanese Constitution and its declaration of government as "a sacred trust" and the notions of "peace for all time" and "banishment of tyranny and slavery" (Constitution of Japan, 1947).

Our reading led to a substantive discussion about the intents and contexts of both documents and the meaning of them today. For example, as we were reading the Japanese Constitution out loud, the Japanese students commented that we were reading it with too much enthusiasm and with an inflated sense of "personality." They said that we were reading it in an American kind of way. And they pointed out that the document indeed uses the language of "peace," "justice and faith," "the banishment of tyranny and slavery," and "sacred trust," more American than Japanese ideals, as this was a postwar constitution that was written largely for the United States and by General Douglas MacArthur, head of the Allied occupation in Japan after World War II. Their comments raised questions about how much a product of Japanese culture and values the Constitution really is.

At the end of class, I told the students that for the next week, we would read Martin Luther King Jr.'s final speech, given in Memphis, Tennessee, on April 3, 1968. I told them we would also read a speech by Robert Kennedy given on the night of King's assassination and that we would read them both aloud.

After class, as I was leaving, I noticed that the students stayed in the hall. I turned to ask if everything was okay. Yuko explained that they were all getting together for dinner that evening just to "hang out." She asked if I wanted to join. I thanked them, but said no, they should enjoy their time together.

Session V

The round began with students reflecting on midterm exams. Midterms produced a great deal of stress in everyone. Each student took a turn discussing concerns—fears that they might not be living up to their own expectations, worries about what underperformance would mean.

Mona offered her own perspective on the pressure of exams. "I feel bad sitting in a class with several hundred other students knowing that some of us are going to do well and others are not. The reality is that in order for me to do well, others have to not do well—that we are in competition with one another. This is all so silly because we all work so hard and want the same things."

This was all quite familiar to the students from Japan, as several of the students had attended "cram schools" in addition to high school.

Yuko described cram school. "I went to cram school at 5:30 after school, and sometimes it ended at 9:30 at night. This depends on what cram school you go to. For me it was mostly math that I studied where you drill down in the information and just sit there and take notes while the teacher talks to you in a small group. You prepare for entrance exams and tests. At first I hated it, and then I realized it helped. In my cram school we were forced to tell everyone our exam score and we were seated accordingly in the class, according to our scores. Summer was the worst. In my 40 days of summer, 39 were filled with cram school to catch up to the best students."

The students discussed their beliefs about grading on a curve and the pressure they felt to have their lives figured out and to excel in school—whether they would go to medical school or graduate school, become teachers, lawyers, or policy makers. No one was completely sure of what the future held, but there was an abiding sense that they were supposed to know soon.

Daniel, a freshman from eastern Washington, laughed and declared, "For now I just want to get through midterms!"

Multiple dimensions of the students' lives were beginning to emerge, ranging from spiritual formation to ethnic identity—all buttressed by heavy pressure to succeed.

We turned our attention to the readings for the day. I introduced Martin Luther King Jr.'s final speech. I was mindful that students in Japan might not have the context for understanding the civil rights movement in the United States or even to whom King was speaking or why. I tried to articulate the racial divisions in the United States—segregated schools, segregated communities, racial hatred, poverty, and mistrust. I described King as a young preacher called to be a part of the movement for voting and civil rights—that he had become an advocate and spokesperson for the movement at a very young age. The students took turns reading the first 10 paragraphs of King's speech aloud. I asked for their reflections.

Mona said, "As many times that I've heard this speech, I've never really read or paid attention to the very beginning, where he imagines moving through time and visiting with Plato, Aristotle, Aristophanes, Lincoln and moving to the modern day."

Yuko asked, "Would you say that things are different in this country now for people of different races?"

I was struck by the question. I was also abundantly aware that the students from Japan were in the United States during another profound racial moment in U.S. history. Michael Brown had just been killed in Ferguson, Missouri; Eric Garner in Staten Island, New York; and 12-year-old Tamir Rice in Cleveland, Ohio, and the images from these deaths seemed to be streaming constantly in the news and through social networks. We all agreed that the United States had a long way to go before reaching the loftiness of the ideals that guide our national rhetoric.

I set the context for Robert Kennedy's speech about Dr. King's assassination. I told the students that Kennedy was a senator from New York and was campaigning for the 1968 presidential nomination when he learned that King had been killed. He gave his speech in Indianapolis, and many in the crowd had not heard the news of King's death. We read his speech aloud.

Yuko asked, "I take from his words and from our discussion that Kennedy was White?"

I was chagrined that I had assumed that the students from Japan would know this. I explained to the students that he was, indeed, White and asked if this shaped their understanding of the speech in any way.

In this speech, Robert Kennedy compared the death of Dr. King to the death of his brother, President John Kennedy, quoting his favorite poem by Aeschylus. We discussed how this poem was both beautiful and terrible for Kennedy and whether there was a poem or meaningful phrase that we held onto in moments of challenge or difficulty.

Hiro wondered aloud whether Kennedy's invoking the death of his brother was an appropriate thing to do in the presence of the profound loss Dr. King represented. He raised the question of whether the meanings of their deaths were similar. I took great joy in feeling that we had created the kind of space where these students could ask these questions about our history.

After a brief yet astoundingly deep conversation about the intersections of empathy, loss, grief, and words that heal us and help others heal, we brought the session to a close. I asked the students to consider the values that most guide their beliefs about leadership.

I told the students that in the next session we would discuss another significant figure in the United States who perhaps had relevance throughout the world. I asked the students to read the words of Catherine Elizabeth Brewer Benson. I handed them an image of her diploma—known to be the first woman's diploma—awarded in July 1840 by Georgia Female College, later called Wesleyan College. I asked the students to consider the relevance of Benson's diploma and of the diploma as a document for us today, whether we reside in the United States or Japan.

Session VI

We began the day with our round. The groups seemed particularly tired today. We discussed the importance of self-care at this point in the quarter.

Lani began our discussion. "I am beginning to wonder whether I should register for the next quarter or if I should take some time off until I am better prepared."

When asked why he was considering such a big decision so early in the year, he replied, "I don't know if I mentioned but my family isn't very well off, and my father has an illness that has limited his mobility. I am just not sure if I should stay in school and ask them to pay so much when I am not completely sure of what I want to do when I finish."

When his classmates pressed him on whether stopping out now was the right decision, he framed the matter as an ethical one. "I don't think this is about what is best for me. I really like it here and want to continue on. The bigger question for me is whether my family can afford to have me move through UW without knowing what I want to do. I think this is an ethical question for me, and I am not sure doing what I am doing is the right thing."

Lani's mind seemed to move between his obligation to self and to his family. This seemed a set of heavy burdens to bear in the first weeks of the quarter—the expectation that he have his path figured out and also have a plan to care for his family. I wondered how many freshmen in our university were straddling borders between home, campus life, academic expectations, and an uncertain future.

We discussed Benson's diploma and the meaning of a diploma in both countries. Why do we have them? What do they mean? How do we know we have earned them, and what do they enable us to say or not say about ourselves?

We also discussed the challenge of weighing what is right for the individual against what is right for others. We concluded that leadership has something to do with our capacity to reflect on the well-being of others in the context of our day-to-day lives.

At this point, I asked the students to do some reflective writing on their understanding of leadership in response to two questions: "Who are leaders you most respect? Why?" and "What do you believe to be some tenets of leadership?" We agreed to develop our ideas on leadership further and share our responses in the coming weeks.

Session VIII

We again began the session with cookies. I wanted to lighten the mood a bit, knowing that the students were still taking exams and were deeply immersed in the demands of the quarter. They seemed to be finding their way. The students from Japan were walking with a sense of confidence; they appeared to know their way around campus and had begun to meet a few of their U.S. classmates. The dialogue in class was moving naturally among the students—not solely prompted by or deferential to me. They were talking to one another and pushing deeper with questions when intriguing thoughts were expressed.

Beginning the round, Hiro said, "I realized something today when I woke up. I realized that the feelings I have been having—these feelings of depression have not been going away. I noticed that I have been feeling this way for a few weeks now. This was an important insight for me, and I should probably do something different now. Thank you for listening."

Hiro often ended his comments with a "thank you for listening." This time, however, the "thank you" at the end of his statement seemed a bit startling.

Yuko implored him to say more. Hiro answered, "I don't mean to offend or surprise you. I just noticed that I have just been feeling blue and that I have been feeling this way for a few weeks. I was hoping it would go away, but it hasn't."

Melissa responded, "That was a really courageous thing to say."

Yuko offered a Japanese perspective. "This is really hard for us to say these things being from Japan and really hard for men to say."

I asked Hiro if we could have permission to carry on with this conversation, showing care for him but also addressing an issue that seemed so important to students in both the United States and Japan. With his permission, I asked why this would be a hard conversation to have among students.

Hiro answered, "There is a lot of pressure on young people and on adults in Japan to be successful. Sometimes the pressure is more than people can handle. I think that is why the suicide rate is so high in our country."

The students handled this conversation with great care. Each shared experiences of sadness, expressing concern for Hiro and making thoughtful suggestions that ranged from careful monitoring to ensuring that his sadness didn't last too long or become too severe. The students were discussing an issue common to college students. Recent surveys have found that depression is one of the most common complaints among college students (Cooperative Institutional Research Program, 2014), yet far too few students seek or find support on their campuses to relieve their symptoms. I presumed that this was especially true for international students.

Hiro reminded me once again of the complexity of the student experience—the intersection of culture, ethnicity, and gender; the challenge of students asking big questions and experiencing transition, yet making their way; and the courage that experience requires. We ended the session discussing campus resources and agreed that care for ourselves and care for each other were invaluable resources.

In preparation for the final session, Hiro asked if he could lead a discussion about the life of Chiune Sugihara, a graduate of a Japanese university, who served as a vice-consul for the Empire of Japan in Lithuania during World War II. With his wife, Yukiko, Sugihara is credited with saving the lives of several thousand Jewish refugees. I agreed that Hiro should introduce Sugihara to the class.

Session IX

Yuko began our weekly round with a statement about self-discovery. "I learned this week and over the past few weeks that I am a woman, that I am a woman of color, and that I have many rights."

I asked her how this came to be a revelation and why she found this so relevant now. She replied, "I have been taking a class on race, gender, and ethnicity, and we have been using these terms, terms that I haven't used before. I've found the class to be really interesting for me personally, that I can describe myself this way. I guess I should have always known this, but I never really said this out loud before."

Yuko seemed to capture the intersection of race, gender, power, and culture. She also took notable pride in her ability to find her voice, to find the words to describe the intricacy of her young life. She seemed to feel safe and confident. Her peers stopped shy of applauding her.

Session X

To begin our final round, Hiro spoke of the pride he felt knowing that Sugihara was a national hero and a graduate from his own university. He seemed to be in much better spirits than in the previous weeks. He gave a brief description of Sugihara's life, the life of a leader.

After Hiro spoke, I offered a summary. I told the class that I was grateful that they allowed me to walk with them on this path through the first 10 weeks of their quarter and their college experience. I referred to our readings and suggested that Galileo, Copernicus, Darwin, and the other 15 figures above Suzzallo Library were fellow travelers, as were Martin Luther King Jr., Robert Kennedy, Catherine Elizabeth Brewer Benson, and Chiune and Yukiko Sugihara. I posited that the U.S. Bill of Rights and the Japanese Constitution symbolized values of our respective nations as well as values that might guide their educations and desires for leadership throughout their lives. I thanked the students for how they trusted one another and shared their challenges, fears, aspirations, and lived experiences.

Conclusion: What I Learned

So much of our students' college experience requires them to learn about others' experience and knowledge. I wanted to provide this cross-cultural group of new students with an opportunity to place their own experience alongside that of others. In the process, they learned something about themselves as leaders, as members of distinct groups that often overlapped, and as people who shared common responses to experience, such as the anxiety around exams and the need to succeed in the eyes of others.

I learned, once again, that students are constantly engaged in complex forms of inquiry about themselves, about their fields of study. They are always thinking about where they are and why. Also, I saw that they have a depth of compassion and caring about life matters that isn't reflected in how they carry themselves or their young ages and is rarely talked about in our courses. My assumptions about these students were constantly being challenged. I knew that they were caring, but I underestimated just how much they cared. I knew they experienced stress, but I underestimated just how much stress they experienced. I knew they were learning, but I underestimated the depth and range of their early learning experiences on campus.

The joy I felt when I overheard these students, all of whom were exceptional high school students, discussing things that we easily take for granted—a new bus route, their first American college football game, academic successes, and even first encounters with academic insecurity—I underestimated this as well.

Note

1. Names and sometimes genders of students have been changed to protect their privacy.

References

Bakhtin, M. M. (1981). *The dialogic imagination: Four essays.* Austin: University of Texas Press.

Ballenger, C. (1997). Social identities, moral narratives, scientific argumentation: Science talk in a bilingual classroom. *Language and Education, 11,* 1–14.

Beyer, C. H., Gillmore, G. M., & Fisher, A. T. (2007). *Inside the undergraduate experience.* San Francisco, CA: Jossey-Bass.

Constitution of Japan. (1947). Preamble, ¶ 1 and 2. Retreived from http://afe.easia .columbia.edu/ps/japan/constitution_1947.pdf

Cooperative Institutional Research Program, UCLA Higher Education Research Institute. (2014). *The American freshman: National norms fall 2014.* Retrieved from http://www.heri.ucla.edu/monographs/TheAmericanFreshman2014.pdf

Kim, Y. Y. (2005). Adapting to a new culture: An integrative communication theory. In W. B. Gudykunst (Ed.), *Theorizing about intercultural communication* (pp. 375–400). Thousand Oaks, CA: Sage.

Kuh, G. D. (2008). *High-impact educational practices: What they are, who has access to them, and why they matter.* Washington, DC: Association of American Colleges and Universities.

Rydell, R. J., McConnell, A. R., & Beilock, S.L. (2009). Multiple social identities and stereotype threat: Imbalance, accessibility, and working. *Memory Journal of Personality and Social Psychology, 5,* 949–966.

THE INTERSECTION OF LIFE AND LEARNING

What Cultural Wealth and Liberal Education Mean for Whole Student Development

Ashley Finley and Tia McNair

Higher education, almost by definition, is an intersection. At its core is the coming together of disciplines, diverse interests and perspectives, communities, present problems, and future aspirations. Students standing at this intersection may not immediately or fully see the transformative convergence of this core with their lived experiences or grasp the influence these intersections might have on the people they will become. Yet it is precisely at this juncture that one's knowledge and the filtering of that knowledge through multiple lenses lead to broader understanding, learning, awareness, and agency. Through processes of exploration and examination to challenge and define truth and through sense making because of or despite confusion, students at the intersection of life and learning do not just learn. They learn who they are.

In this chapter, we explore how the process of learning—the *way* students learn—is central to personal and civic identity formation. However, equally critical but often overlooked is the ability of students' learning to reveal and deepen a sense of who they are and hope to be in the world. The process of discovery in learning is about not only revealing ideas but also the revealing of a student's position in relationship to those ideas, how his or her background and life circumstances come to bear on that understanding, and awaking to the belief that understanding can empower him or her to respond—intellectually, civically, and emotionally. The promise of discovery for *all* students, however, is best realized through the acknowledgment of the unique qualities and ways of knowing that *each* student brings to learning.

Intentionally integrating and applying students' lived experience—their cultural wealth—to deepen connection with and comprehension of learning are, perhaps, the richest resources students have. Valuing cultural wealth is particularly meaningful for students who have been historically marginalized in higher education and who may feel silenced in the classroom,

Regardless of background, learning and identity development are at the heart of Aristotle's notion of "the examined life"—the idea that what makes us wholly functioning beings is the ability to inquire, to reflect, and to situate ourselves within a larger social context. The philosophy of a liberal education, the guiding paradigm for much of American higher education, is both the extension and practical application of Aristotle's emphasis on a life of inquiry. But the freedom to inquire is intimately bound with the reality of one's existence, particularly within a civic context. A true liberal education for all students is, therefore, attentive to learning as a source of personal development *and* of the development of students' civic identities. As one scholar has noted,

> College can be a crucial shaping environment for the development of moral identity and civic identity—if educational opportunities deliberately engage students in accordance with his or her developmental readiness. We must be mindful of this need as we work to create more purposeful, deliberate, and connected educational experiences for our students. (Knefelkamp, 2008)

What follows is a closer look at how learning can be connected to students' personal and civic development. Guided by the tenets of liberal education, this examination is practically grounded in the words of students themselves to provide an authentic account of what identity and learning mean in the twenty-first century. This means also carefully considering how educational experiences invite and build upon the assets of *each* student's cultural wealth, a critical means by which students, particularly underserved students, can connect learning to their lives and lived experiences to better understand who they are and strive to be.

We then explore strategies for campus action and inquiry that can more wholly and inclusively support students' personal and civic identity development. Beginning with practices commonly referred to as "high-impact" (e.g., service-learning, experiences with diversity, learning communities), we consider how quality design elements of these practices can encourage student growth and identity formation. We also provide the critical questions educators can ask themselves to reflect upon the degree to which quality designed learning environments also build upon the strengths of students' cultural wealth. Finally, the alignment of high-impact practices with formational elements of civic identity is addressed to understand how the intersection of life and learning can holistically connect who students are with their role as civic agents.

In Their Own Words: Student Expressions of Learning and Identity Development

Expressions of Agency as Part of Identity Development

The following quotes are drawn from focus groups conducted with approximately 100 underserved students (i.e., underrepresented minority, first-generation, low-income, and transfer students) in three states at nine four-year public universities (see Finley & McNair, 2013). The focus of the research study, broadly aimed at understanding how students articulate the effects and meaning of their learning, illuminated the very real ways in which learning provided students a sense of empowerment, agency, and civic identity. Specifically, when asked to talk about the learning experiences that most stood out to them and why, students very often drew connections between how their learning environment helped to facilitate a sense of self-worth and empowerment. In some cases empowerment came from making connections that inspired feelings of elation and happiness:

> It's like a joy that comes over you because all of a sudden you're studying, and you're going over it . . . and all of a sudden, it's like a light comes on. (student in Wisconsin)

A similar excitement arose when students understood that they were engaging deeply with certain material:

> I'm usually pretty excited and passionate about it, and when I go home and do my homework, I'm really enjoying it so I think the joy really tells [that] you're liking it and engaged. (student in Oregon)

Students also referenced agency in terms of their ability to connect learning, with an awareness of being able to succeed, both in college and in life:

> There is no organization or professor to hold your hand [after college] and doing [some] of these things on your own lets you know that you can do that . . . you can't help anybody unless you can actually do it yourself in the first place. So I think [college provides] empowerment of knowing I can do this. This is what I'm capable of, and having that awareness gives you the courage to do other things and keep moving. (student in Wisconsin)

Students' articulations of agency were also present in comments about pushing themselves to seek out new experiences, find additional sources of information, or act on curiosity:

> I . . . feel like in high school, I was always waiting around to be told what to study versus (in college) it's kind of like I have an idea and I know how I can make that idea into some sort of academic project to better society. . . . I feel like that's incredibly important for students to be able to do. (student in Wisconsin)

Another student echoed this sentiment, noting that fully understanding the material sometimes requires steps beyond completing the assignment:

> I don't want to give up on something just because my assignment is done, and, you know, my curiosity is what is going to keep me going from now until whenever next graduation . . . it's helped me learn that I do have that level of, you know . . . inquisitive enough to keep pursuing what I really want to do. (student in California)

Focus-group conversations also revealed dimensions of agency that may be particularly salient for the growth and identity development of underserved students. Because these students are often the first in their families to attend college, they may lack crucial support networks that provide reassurance and encouragement as students make their way through college. As one underserved student commented,

> I grew up thinking that I couldn't be [in college], but here I am now doing all this, and so [being here] made me realize my self-worth, and that I could ask abstract questions, and I could go out and find answers to them, and then tell other people about it who are also wondering the same thing that I'm wondering. (student in Oregon)

Expressions of Civic Identity as Part of Personal Development

Students, as citizens who interact with various communities during the college experience, seek educators who can help them develop the intellectual *and* the civic capacities to be part of the collective, while still valuing the aspects of self that define *individual identity*. Students' expressions of how learning had impacted their personal development reinforced this idea. Their sense of themselves was about who they were as individuals, as well as who they were in relationship to others. They expressed a desire to share their learning with others and to be a part of a larger community, whether that community was made up of other students, a community beyond the campus walls, or the larger world. For example, one student described how group-based learning environments helped foster an ethic of caring for the shared understanding and learning among fellow classmates:

> So it makes you just, when you see your peers around, like, "Hey, how are you doing?" You know, "Did you do good on that test?" Or you want to make sure . . . that you guys are all on the same page, and if somebody doesn't understand, you be like, "You don't get it? All right, let me show you real fast." . . . . If we're a group, we're supposed to stick together. (student in Wisconsin)

As a student in Oregon commented, a sense of civic identity can emerge from gaining an understanding of one's place in the world: "It's not just, hey, I've got to do something; it's *I want to do something*, and *I want to make a difference in the world*" (emphasis added).

Finally, focus-group comments also reflected how students' civic identity was shaped by connecting learning with a desire to give back to their local communities:

> [My service-learning experiences] really made me want to be an activist and work with people [to] provide what services and knowledge I have for people who may be lacking that . . . it just really helped me figure out what I want to do with my life, and . . . where I wanted to guide my knowledge to better serve my community. (student in California)

> My community is very important to me so having a degree in nursing would allow me to be able to help not only my community but also people in other regions of the United States, perhaps the world. (student in Wisconsin)

Recognizing Cultural Wealth as an Asset for Identity Development

Reflective practice has long been understood as an essential practice for deepening learning (e.g., see Bass, 2012; Rodgers, 2002). But reflection is also a vital tool for personal development. Reflection provides the opportunity for students to draw upon their life experiences, make connections between experience and content, and apply what they've learned to issues that are meaningful to their lives. It is through this process that concepts and theories often gain real-world significance and become more relevant. However, for reflection to be an effective practice for *all* students, each student must feel acknowledged, validated, and understood. This means intentionally making the diversity of students' experiences a part of discussion and applicable to course material.

The concepts of cultural capital and, more specifically, cultural wealth are useful for understanding how each student's background and viewpoint can be maximized, deepening understanding and reflection and building inclusive learning environments. *Cultural capital* is "the general cultural background, knowledge, disposition, and skills that are passed on from one generation to another" (McLaren, 1994, p. 219). The notion of *cultural wealth*, however, reframes traditional notions of cultural capital to emphasize the knowledge and experiences that students, particularly students of color, bring with them to the classroom and to learning environments as crucial resources for themselves and for others to help deepen understanding (Yosso, 2005). When encountering new knowledge or learning experiences, students of color can draw upon certain cultural assets, such as language, their desire to succeed, familial and other social supports, and openness to diversity, to make connections to their lives and provide real-world applications for subject matter (see Rendón, Nora, & Kanagala, 2014).

The following quotes are from interviews that were conducted as part of a grant to investigate underserved students' perspectives on general education. They revealed how the ability to share aspects of one's cultural wealth helped to deepen personal connections in the classroom and allowed students to feel more understood and accepted:

> My professor, he used to ask . . . [about] our personal experience, like what do we think about [a topic] and . . . if we have faced anything like this? . . . When I was talking, people get to know my culture . . . what I faced or my opinion . . . they get to know better my culture, my religion, everything. (student in Texas)

> I look forward to going to classes where teachers respect you and they're open to [listening] to your opinions, and . . . allow [students] to contribute their personal background, and [promote] cultural diversity in the classroom. Those are the classes I think that are fun . . . and I learn a lot. (student in Texas)

Faculty can contribute to students' ability to make meaning of what they learn by teaching in ways that are culturally responsive and that invite students to explore their cultural and experiential assets. These forms of cultural wealth are vital to the identity development of diverse groups of students, and should be viewed as assets, not deficits, toward enhancing the processes of both teaching and learning.

Campus Action: Quality Educational Designs and Critical Questions

The Role of Quality High-Impact Practices to Promote Identity and Civic Development

If higher education represents an intersection of multiple disciplines, diverse interests and perspectives, and communities, how can educators help all students explore, discover, and define their evolving identities as participants in this community? What are our individual responsibilities in designing institutional structures, policies, and practices that encourage continual inquiry, build on students' cultural capital as well as ways of knowing, and promote deep levels of engagement with learning? How deliberate are educators in the design of educational experiences for students that address their individual readiness, knowledge, and purpose to promote student agency? To address these questions, we offer the following educational design recommendations and pose critical questions that are necessary for all educators, both faculty and staff, to answer in developing learning environments that can serve as building blocks for student discovery and self-realization.

As part of the Association of American Colleges and Universities' Liberal Education and America's Promise initiative, and in partnership with the National Survey of Student Engagement, identifying so-called high-impact educational practices has been and continues to be an avenue for addressing how to create deliberate educational designs that are purposeful, connect to students' lived experiences, and promote student learning and engagement. These practices include, but are not limited to, first-year experiences, common intellectual experiences, learning communities, writing-intensive courses, collaborative assignments and projects, undergraduate research, diversity/global learning, service-learning, community-based learning, internships, and capstone courses and projects. The term *high-impact* comes from the evidence that students who participate in these practices, especially underserved students, have increased retention, persistence, and completion rates as well as higher self-reported learning gains compared to students who do not participate (see Finley & McNair, 2013; Kuh, 2008; Kuh & O'Donnell, 2013). The quality design elements of these practices, along with an awareness of who students are and characteristics of civic identity strategies, can help students develop a sense of what matters to them and how they can situate themselves to address those matters.

For years, campus educators have been utilizing those educational practices labeled high-impact. The focus of scholarship, more recently, has been on the quality characteristics of these practices in helping students to demonstrate achievement of defined learning outcomes. The ability of these practices to foster identity development for personal and social development is a natural extension of the inherent design and function of these practices when implemented well. Kuh and O'Donnell (2013) identified the following eight key elements of quality high-impact practices:

1. Performance expectations set at appropriately high levels
2. Significant investment of time and effort by students over an extended period of time
3. Interactions with faculty and peers about substantive matters
4. Experiences with diversity, wherein students are exposed to and must contend with people and circumstances that differ from those with which students are familiar
5. Frequent, timely, and constructive feedback
6. Periodic, structured opportunities to reflect and integrate learning
7. Opportunities to discover relevance of learning through real-world applications
8. Public demonstration of competence (p. 10)

Educators who are seeking to design high-impact practices should evaluate the levels at which their educational practices are addressing these key elements. For example, what are the expectations for student learning associated with participation in a learning community, service-learning experience, internship, or undergraduate research experience? How are students investing significant time and effort in a substantive, real-world problem that reflects their interests and lived experiences? How are students encouraged to explore diverse perspectives and to engage in self-examination as part of the educational experience? Are there opportunities for reflection and constructive feedback? How can students integrate the learning from this experience with other growth opportunities? What opportunities are available for students to share their knowledge with others?

Connecting High-Impact Practices With Students' Cultural Wealth and Civic Identities

Integrating these elements of quality high-impact practice design with knowledge of students' cultural wealth and/or cultural capital can serve as the foundation for creating a learning environment where students from diverse backgrounds have the freedom to inquire, to learn, and to explore their evolving identities. As previously discussed, understanding who students are and the assets they bring to their higher education experiences is critically important to the educational design process. High-impact practices that integrate knowledge of student interests and cultural backgrounds can have a significant influence on identity development and personal growth. Building on the cultural wealth theory proposed by Yosso (2005) and expanded by Rendón et al. (2014), educators should continually ask, "How does the design of this educational practice value the diversity of student experiences and cultural backgrounds? How does the educational design utilize the lessons gained from student perseverance and the ability to navigate multiple, diverse worlds? How can the educational experiences build on students' strong commitment to community responsibility and social change?"

Identifying the intersections of the quality elements of high-impact practice design and civic identity characteristics with a clear understanding of who students are can provide an opportunity for campuses to develop educational experiences that can be transformative for students. Knefelkamp (2008) outlined four elements of civic identity:

1. Civic identity does not develop in isolation. It develops over time *through engagement with others* who bring a wide variety of interpretations, life experiences, and characteristics to any discussion of moral dilemmas. It develops in the context of engaging the real social, political, and economic structures within any given society or culture.
2. Civic identity is not the same as, but is deeply connected to, *complex intellectual and ethical development.* Thus the work of helping students become more intellectually complex expands their capacity to think and act as citizens.
3. Civic identity is a *holistic practice.* It requires an integration of critical thinking and the capacity for empathy. It challenges us to identify with others who may be significantly different from ourselves while acting consistently in the face of unexpected circumstances.
4. Civic identity becomes a *deliberately chosen and repeatedly enacted aspect of the self.* Like any other identity status, civic identity requires active reflection and experimentation. (pp. 2–3)

The intersections of Knefelkamp's characteristics of civic identity development and the quality design elements for high-impact practices raise important considerations for developing integrative educational designs that advance learning and promote self-discovery. The notion that civic identity development does not progress in isolation also applies to the implementation of high-impact practices. Quality high-impact practices that seek to promote identity development and incorporate students' cultural capital and cultural wealth should be integrated across the curriculum and the cocurriculum in order to provide avenues for full engagement and participation by students, faculty, and staff.

By focusing on both identity and civic development as holistic processes, educators can intentionally design educational practices that reflect the goals of a liberal education while helping students explore and reflect on the aspects of their identity that will enable all students to fully participate in our democracy. The value of these learning designs as conduits primarily for students' intellectual growth should not overshadow the inherent, and equally important, value of designing high-impact practices that reinforce the importance of being a scholar and a citizen. Transformative learning environments that push boundaries, embrace difference, and help shape students' identities are our responsibility and our calling as educators. As Butler (2014) put it,

> Through our research and teaching, we educators can foster inclusion of the varied manifestations of diversity in our students and our courses, grappling with difference and sameness not as conundrums, but as synergistic and intersecting dynamics that reveal the human experience and ways to improve it. (p. 6)

Conclusion

The intersection of life and learning for students is not a wholly comfortable one. They will by turns be challenged, exasperated, and perhaps even a bit disillusioned. But the promise of a liberal education is in taking seriously students' development for the sake of who they are and will be as citizens, free thinkers, and architects of their future.

The promise of a liberal education in the twenty-first century is also the keen awareness that all students must have access to the opportunities and bounties reaped from the introspection, knowledge seeking, and meaning making necessary for identity development. The concept of cultural wealth reminds us that *all* students, particularly those traditionally underserved by higher education, bring assets to bear on their exploration of identity. In inclusive learning environments, students with varied sources of cultural wealth have the opportunity to share with one another in the interest of gaining greater perspective on the world around them and the people with whom they share communities.

As highlighted in the second part of this chapter, educators and institutions have the responsibility and power to shape programs and policies in ways that invite students, regardless of their background, to explore what is meaningful to them as learners and as social actors. It does, however, require careful, deliberate creation of learning environments, culturally responsive teaching, and a recognition that students do not just learn on college campuses. They learn who they are.

References

Bass, R. (2012). Disrupting ourselves: The problem of learning in higher education. *Educause Review, 47*(2), 23–33.

Butler, J. (2014). Replacing the cracked mirror: The challenge for diversity and inclusion. *Diversity & Democracy, 17*(4), 6.

Finley, A., & McNair, T. (2013). *Assessing underserved students' engagement in high-impact practices.* Washington, DC: Association of American Colleges and Universities.

Knefelkamp, L. L. (2008). Civic identity: Locating self in community. *Diversity & Democracy, 11*(2), 2.

Kuh, G. (2008). *High-impact educational practices: What they are, who has access to them, and why they matter.* Washington, DC: Association of American Colleges and Universities.

Kuh, G., & O'Donnell, K. (2013). *Ensuring quality and taking high-impact practices to scale.* Washington, DC: Association of American Colleges and Universities.

McLaren, P. (1994). *Life in schools: An introduction to critical pedagogy in the foundations of education.* New York, NY: Longman.

Rendón, L. I., Nora, A., & Kanagala, V. (2014). *Ventajas/assets conocimientos/knowledge: Leveraging Latin@ strengths to foster student success.* San Antonio, TX: Center for Research and Policy in Education.

Rodgers, C. (2002). Seeing student learning: Teacher change and the role of reflection. *Harvard Educational Review, 72*(2), 230–253.

Yosso, T. J. (2005). Whose culture has capital? A critical race theory discussion of community cultural wealth. *Race Ethnicity and Education, 8*(1), 69–91.

CONCLUSION

Guiding Principles for Working at the Intersections

Brooke Barnett and Peter Felten

Intersectionality emphasizes the importance of connections and relationships, rather than attending primarily to isolated and individual factors, like race or gender. Intersectional theorists maintain that to understand a situation, we must focus on the dynamic linkages across difference. This is as true for groups as it is for individuals. A person's well-being rests in part on the capacity to connect the various parts of his or her identity into a coherent whole. Similarly, a community's strength and resilience are contingent on the relationships among groups and individuals within that community. By attending to these intersections, this theoretical approach provides a clear lens for critically examining campus climates and organizational structures in higher education.

While an intersectionality framework is academic and theoretical, it is also practical and action-oriented. Intersectional analysis promotes action toward a more just society (Dill & Zambrana, 2009). As such, it should serve as a foundation for essential work in higher education, including effective and ethical student and colleague recruitment, bias response and prevention, academic innovation, student support, and curricular learning.

By exploring intersectionality in action, the preceding chapters prompt us to ask how our campuses, and our own work, might be different if approached from an intersectional perspective. While the particular answers to that question will vary depending on campus climate, institutional mission and role, and a host of other factors, we propose five guiding principles that apply to any campus.

Intersectional Work Connects Multiple and Varied Aspects of Campus Life

Too often, higher education initiatives for diversity and inclusion operate in distinct and separate areas. Typical silos include the core curriculum, student affairs, admissions, and human resources. While these are essential partners in such work, intersectionality reminds us that this is common work. Individuals and groups that might not be among "the usual suspects" can and should play vital roles in creating inclusive excellence. For instance, campus architects and planners can design accessible spaces that encourage both formal and informal interactions. Academic affairs administrators can advocate for interdisciplinary and intersectional scholarship and can invest in inclusive pedagogies across all disciplines. Student life staff can partner with faculty to develop an intellectual and inclusive community that counters stereotype threat and that makes interaction across difference a cultural norm. Campus safety officers can use community-policing principles and practices to develop strong relationships with students. These and other actions are helpful on their own but are particularly powerful when conducted in concert. Successful higher education institutions approach diversity work across all constituents by focusing on major aspects of human difference, enacting comprehensive strategic plans focused on learning for everyone in the community, and creating a campus climate where all members can thrive.

Intersectional Work Deeply Engages Communities and Content

Engagement with diversity and inclusion should be woven into the fabric of your campus. Strengthening that fabric entails attending to both the horizontal threads that reach across campus and the vertical ones that go deeply into one area or topic (Keeling, Underhile, & Wall, 2007). Serious encounters with difference require the kind of careful and critical analysis that is possible only with immersion. Often in higher education, that immersion comes from an academic discipline, and faculty serve as mentors and guides as students struggle and learn. At other times, students (or faculty and staff) are immersed in a community that provides them a depth of experience and insight. In this case, professional staff or wise peers offer the support and challenge necessary to persist through difficulty in order to learn.

Integrating students' (or others') learning around human differences across multiple experiences creates new meaning and insights, more proficient transfer of knowledge to new situations, and greater adaptability in the real world. When a student's studies in a major and the core curriculum are echoed and amplified in his or her experiences in campus organizations and during community service opportunities, that student is most likely to learn deeply. Tailoring experiences to the particular needs of individuals and groups can further enhance these outcomes. For instance, teaching all students to understand religious and secular traditions and then to navigate within and across these differences not only supports marginalized students on campus but also provides majority students with knowledge, skills, and capacities they will need in their lives after college.

Intersectional Work Develops Individuals and Organizations

A vast and growing body of research has demonstrated that a diverse student body, faculty, and staff increase creativity, innovation, and problem solving, key aspects of a successful twenty-first-century learning environment (e.g., Gurin, Dey, Hurtado, & Gurin, 2002; Gurin, Nagda, & Lopez, 2004; Hurtado, Ruiz Alvarado, & Guillermo-Wann, 2015). Often, campuses have programs to develop the knowledge and capacities of individuals to function in a diverse environment. These programs can be invaluable, but they sometimes fail to achieve their full potential because they do not attend to developing the organization itself. Intersectional analysis can help highlight and ameliorate structural obstacles to equity and inclusion, such as hiring practices or financial aid policies that inadvertently but effectively marginalize certain groups. Cultivating and sustaining a diverse campus requires systematic support for both individual and organizational change (Pope, Reynolds, & Muellers, 2014).

Intersectional Work Asks and Addresses the Critical Questions

Institutions must create robust, iterative, and comprehensive policies, protocols, and approaches to explore issues of diversity and inclusion on campus. Resting on laurels is particularly dangerous in higher education since our student population changes frequently. Colleges and universities should develop processes for collecting and using evidence to monitor campus climate as well as to ensure that all groups have opportunities to be successful. For example, the Wabash-Provost Scholars Program at North Carolina A&T State University trains undergraduates to analyze institutional data (e.g., retention and graduation rates for different student populations), conduct focus groups with peers to better understand the meaning of that information, and then present their findings to campus leaders (Cook-Sather, Bovill, & Felten 2014). Creating space for often unheard voices to enter the conversation about key institutional questions is one powerful way to remain open to criticism and growth.

Intersectional Work Plans and Acts Based on Values and Commitments

Your campus commitment needs to be rooted in institutional mission and values. Your goals must be clear not only in making strategic decisions and setting priorities, but also in daily activities across campus. If you wait until a bias incident occurs to articulate the importance of diversity and inclusion, you will be on the defensive. By being explicit and consistent, you will not only have a solid foundation for action in the moment but also help create cultural norms that support and encourage positive interactions across difference.

This is exciting, challenging, and crucial work. Be prepared to commit for the long haul. At times, change will be incremental, or you may seem to be slipping backward. However, when your work draws on clear institutional commitments, you will have a firm anchor no matter how rough the waters become. And when you focus on the intersections on campus, you will construct a powerful network that will support diversity and inclusion both today and for years to come.

References

Cook-Sather, A., Bovill, C., & Felten, P. (2014). *Engaging students as partners in learning and teaching: A guide for faculty.* San Francisco, CA: Jossey-Bass.

Gurin, P., Dey, E. L., Hurtado, S., & Gurin, G. (2002). Diversity and higher education: Theory and impact on educational outcomes. *Harvard Educational Review, 72*(3), 330–366.

Gurin, P., Nagda, B. A., & Lopez, G. E. (2004). The benefits of diversity in education for democratic citizenship. *Journal of Social Issues, 60*, 17–34. doi:10.1111/j.0022-4537.2004.00097.x

Keeling, R. P., Underhile, R., & Wall, A. F. (2007). Horizontal and vertical structures: The dynamics of organization in higher education. *Liberal Education, 93*(4), 22–31.

Pope, R. L., Reynolds, A. L., & Mueller, J. A. (2014). *Creating multicultural change on campus.* San Francisco, CA: Jossey-Bass.

EDITORS AND CONTRIBUTORS

Brooke Barnett is associate provost for inclusive community and professor of communications at Elon University, where she leads university efforts in diversity and global engagement and cultural and special programs. Her research focuses on mass communication law, media effects, and diversity and inclusion on college campuses.

Nancy L. Chick is a university chair in teaching and learning, academic director of the Taylor Institute for Teaching and Learning, and a tenured faculty member in the English department at the University of Calgary. She is also founding coeditor of the journal *Teaching & Learning Inquiry.*

Jon Dooley is assistant vice president for student life, dean of campus life, and assistant professor at Elon University. He is responsible for several offices and university initiatives for diversity and inclusion, civic engagement and service-learning, and the integration of residential and academic student experiences.

Peter Felten is assistant provost for teaching and learning, director of the Center for Engaged Learning, and professor of history at Elon University. His publications include *Transforming Students: Fulfilling the Promise of Higher Education* (Johns Hopkins University Press, 2014) and *Engaging Students as Partners in Learning and Teaching* (Jossey-Bass, 2014).

Ashley Finley is associate vice president of academic affairs and dean of the Dominican experience at Dominican University of California. She is also national evaluator for the Bringing Theory to Practice project. Her publications include *Civic Learning and Teaching* (Bringing Theory to Practice, 2014) and, with coauthor Tia McNair, *Assessing Underserved Students' Engagement in High-Impact Practices.* (Association of American Colleges & Universities, 2013).

Amy Howard is executive director of the Bonner Center for Civic Engagement and associate faculty in American studies at the University of Richmond. She is the author of *More Than Shelter: Activism and Community in San Francisco Public Housing* (University of Minnesota Press, 2014). Howard also serves on the City of Richmond Planning Commission.

Leo M. Lambert is the president of Elon University. He has served on the boards of Campus Compact, Project Pericles, and the National Association of Independent Colleges and Universities and has been consistently recognized as a leader in civic engagement and engaged teaching and learning.

Juliette Landphair is the vice president of student affairs at the University of Mary Washington. Her research focuses on two distinct areas: college student development and twentieth-century New Orleans social history. She has published essays in history journals and student affairs journals.

Niki Latino is the executive director of academic resources in student life at the University of Denver. Her research interests include inclusive leadership in higher education and inclusive excellence and diversity. She coauthored the chapter "Ethnic Identity: Unanticipated Consequences" in *Race, Equality, and Teaching* (Trentham Books, 2009).

Lucy LePeau is an assistant professor of higher education and student affairs at Indiana University–Bloomington. Her research, teaching, and service activities have focused on academic affairs and student affairs partnerships promoting diversity and social justice initiatives on campus, organizational change, and improved student affairs practice.

Amanda Lineberry is the community-based learning fellow at the Bonner Center for Civic Engagement. She graduated from the University of Richmond in 2014 with a BA in American studies and political science. She is also in the nonprofit studies graduate program at the University of Richmond's School of Professional and Continuing Studies.

Alta Mauro serves as the founding director of Intercultural Education and Spiritual Life at New York University–Abu Dhabi, where she leads university efforts to strategize around cross- and intercultural competence. She is pursuing a PhD in educational leadership and cultural foundations at the University of North Carolina–Greensboro.

Angela Mazaris is director of the LGBTQ Center and an assistant teaching professor in the women's, gender, and sexuality studies department at Wake Forest University, where she also serves as a member of the Diversity and Inclusion Leadership Team. Her research interests include queer public history projects and student engagement/success.

Michael A. McDonald has been provost at Kalamazoo College since 2008. Prior to that he was a mathematics professor and held various administrative positions at Occidental College.

Tia McNair is the associate vice president for diversity, equity, and student success at the Association of American Colleges and Universities. She is coauthor of *Assessing Underserved Students' Engagement in High-Impact Practices* (AAC&U, 2013) and the lead author of *Becoming a Student-Ready College* (Jossey-Bass, forthcoming).

Paul Parsons is founding dean of the School of Communications at Elon University. The school received the national Equity & Diversity Award from the Association for Education in Journalism and Mass Communication in 2010 for its commitment to gender equity and success in building a diverse faculty. Parsons worked for 10 years as a reporter and editor for United Press International and the Associated Press and holds a PhD in communications. He spent a year as a Fulbright professor in Beijing, China, and a year as a visiting professor in Singapore.

Eboo Patel is president and founder of Interfaith Youth Core, a Chicago-based nonprofit partnering with higher education to advance the civic priority of interfaith cooperation. He holds a doctorate in the sociology of religion from Oxford University, where he studied on a Rhodes scholarship. Patel is the author of *Acts of Faith* (Beacon, 2007), *Sacred Ground: Pluralism, Prejudice, and the Promise of America* (Beacon, 2012), and *Interfaith Leadership: A Primer* (Beacon, forthcoming).

Danielle R. Picard is a PhD candidate in history at Vanderbilt University. She serves as a graduate teaching fellow at Vanderbilt's Center for Teaching, where she teaches graduate students and postdoctoral fellows in the certificate in college teaching program and the annual teaching assistant orientation. She won the Meyers Graduate Teaching Award from the University of Rochester in 2011.

Leigh-Anne Royster is director of the Office of Inclusive Community Well-Being at Elon University, where she oversees the bias and harassment protocols and processes and coordinates diversity education for faculty and staff. With more than 18 years of experience working with violence response and prevention, she also serves on statewide and local boards focused on prevention and response.

Jeff Stein is chief of staff, secretary to the board of trustees, and assistant professor of English at Elon University. He earned his BA from Beloit College and MFA from Colorado State University. He has published poetry as well as articles on service-learning, multifaith initiatives, and creating inclusive campuses.

Ed Taylor is the dean and vice provost of undergraduate academic affairs and a professor of education at the University of Washington. His publications include two coauthored books, *Inside the Undergraduate Teaching Experience: The University of Washington's Growth in Faculty Teaching Study* (SUNY Press, 2013) and *Foundations of Critical Race Theory in Education* (Routledge, forthcoming).

Sarah B. Westfall is vice president for student development and dean of students at Kalamazoo College. She writes about student affairs, small colleges, crisis management, and other interesting things.

Eileen B. Wilson-Oyelaran has been president of Kalamazoo College since July 2005. Her area of professional expertise is cross-cultural child development. She has taught and held administrative positions at Salem College, Winston-Salem State University, and Obafemi Awolowo University in Ile-Ife, Nigeria.

reaching volume. Going beyond acquisition of classic content and skills proficiencies, the kinds of learning this book addresses embrace equally the development of creativity, empathy, and mindfulness, and include the importance of wellness and relaxation in sustaining mental performance. Everyone who touches students in today's institutions—from teaching faculty to student affairs professionals—will find something to learn here."—*Peter T. Ewell, vice president, National Center for Higher Education Management Systems*

"The right book at the right time. This timely and well-constructed book addresses a vital issue facing higher education today: the need to increase critical thinking, communication, creativity, and resilience for today's college graduates. Drawing on neuroscience research and exploring innovations in teaching and learning, this book explores exciting new approaches to improve the outcomes of the college experience. There is really nothing like this in the higher education literature—very impressive."—*Kevin Kruger, president, NASPA–Student Affairs Administrators in Higher Education*

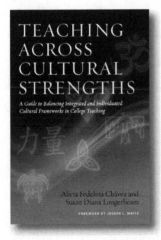

Teaching Across Cultural Strengths

A Guide to Balancing Integrated and Individuated Cultural Frameworks in College Teaching
Alicia Fedelina Chávez, Susan Diana Longerbeam
Foreword by Joseph L. White

"*Teaching Across Cultural Strengths* is an important book that can transform college teaching. It provides a breakthrough approach to addressing the urgent problem of how to effectively teach an increasingly multicultural and international student body now enrolling in our colleges and universities. Beginning with an important question, 'How does my culture manifest itself in my teaching?', the authors take us on a journey of self-discovery. Their objective is to explain why and how to 'balance the application of diverse cultural strengths to deepen student learning through enhancement of teaching and introspection.' The result is a book filled with rich insights, techniques, best practices, and personal stories of success about what works to engage both students and faculty in college classrooms today."—*Roberto Ibarra, associate professor, Department of Sociology and Criminology, University of New Mexico*

22883 Quicksilver Drive
Sterling, VA 20166-2102

Subscribe to our e-mail alerts: www.Styluspub.com

Also available from Stylus

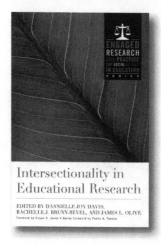

Intersectionality in Educational Research

Edited by Dannielle Joy Davis, Rachelle Brunn-Bevel, and James L. Olive
Foreword by Susan R. Jones
Series Foreword by Penny A. Pasque

"This book offers a comprehensive, complex, and well-organized overview of intersectionality as a tool for critical inquiry and analysis and highlights its usefulness as a theoretical perspective and a qualitative and quantitative methodology. Incorporating examples relevant to a variety of disciplines and considering educational issues that range in relevance from K–12 to higher education, this book is a must-read for policy makers, researchers, educators, administrators, practitioners, advocates, and others vested in understanding the intersections of social disparities such as race, class, and gender and the ways in which such intersections shape the educational experiences and outcomes of marginalized populations. Whether your knowledge of intersectionality reflects that of a novice or seasoned scholar, you will find this book enthralling and the reflective questions at the end of each chapter thought-provoking."—*Yvette Murphy-Erby, associate dean, Fulbright College of Arts and Sciences, University of Arkansas*

"*Intersectionality in Educational Research* is an ambitious book designed to introduce readers to definitions and uses of intersectional theory in studying educational policy, practice, and theory. The editors have brought together scholars who employ intersectional theory in empirical and theoretical projects that span K-12 and higher education, students and faculty, and research approaches. This book is an ideal text for readers seeking to enter the scholarly conversation about intersectionality in education research."—*Kristen Renn, professor of higher, adult, and lifelong education, Department of Educational Administration, Michigan State University*

The Neuroscience of Learning and Development

Enhancing Creativity, Compassion, Critical Thinking, and Peace in Higher Education
Edited by Marilee J. Bresciani Ludvik
Foreword by Gavin W. Henning
Foreword by Ralph Wolff

"It has been almost 20 years since *How People Learn* summarized initial insights from the new discipline of cognitive science, but up to now these insights have not been turned into practical advice about how to improve teaching and learning in college. Bresciani Ludvik and her colleagues admirably remedy this situation with this far-

(Continues on preceding page)